WILDERNESS

by the same author

Blind White Fish in Persia
Sea Never Dry
High Street Africa
Throw Out Two Hands
The Body
The Seasons
The Dangerous Sort
Mato Grosso
Beside The Seaside
Good Beach Guide
The Human Pedigree
Animals On View

WILDERNESS

by

Anthony Smith

London
GEORGE ALLEN & UNWIN
Boston   Sydney

GEORGE ALLEN & UNWIN LTD
40 Museum Street, London WC1A 1LU

© George Allen & Unwin (Publishers) Ltd, 1978

British Library Cataloguing in Publication Data

Smith, Anthony, b.1926
  Wilderness.
  1. Voyages and travels – 1951–
  I. Title
  910′.4   G503

  ISBN 0–04–910063–7

Typeset in 12 on 14 point Garamond by Trade Linotype Limited
and printed in Great Britain by Hazell Watson & Viney Ltd,
Aylesbury, Bucks

This search for wilderness is dedicated to my companions who, in every continent, helped to make the journey the continual pleasure that it proved to be. They receive short shrift in these pages, but I know they will forgive me for focusing on the wilderness, on the empty portions of this planet that gave us all such joy.

I wish also to thank Douglas Botting, traveller with me in many lands, who supplied a dozen of the photographs.

Contents

I *The Size of Wilderness*

Travel and travellers are two things I loathe—and yet here I am, all set to tell the story of my expeditions.
Claude Lévi-Strauss
Siberia is as long as three games of chess in a jet.
Douglas Botting

I love wilderness. I love it despite its discomforts and not because of them. There may be others who welcome biting insects, who relish intense heat or cold, but I do not. I suffer such extremes and, although I do not fail or wither as quickly as some do, the unpleasantness does not go unnoticed. It would be nicer if the great emptinesses of this planet were not so linked with cold, heat, altitude, blood-sucking arthropods, vengeful vegetation, drought, deluge and difficulty. I appreciate that these drawbacks partly explain why wildernesses exist, devoid of people; but I would welcome a body that could disdain mere flies, the blood-letting that often goes with them, or mere differences of temperature. A tree just stands while the heavens rage. I wish, on occasion, I were a tree, apparently impassive to each changing circumstance and not driven frantic whenever, for example, scarcely visible creatures take fiendish liberties.

I love wilderness for the freedom it gives. It gives liberty to go this way or that, to make simple physical mistakes or avoid them,

11

to be unnerved by predators, to fall foul of some wholly natural event, to feel a part of the system and no longer a spectator. This may sound grandiloquent, for I no more than anyone else would wish to be impaled by a falling bough or eaten by a bear. It is just that wilderness, in being able to provide such real disaster, produces every other aspect of that same event. To be alone and see a bear as it looks for food is to see that bear quite differently; a caged creature does not compare. A spread of wild flowers, unplanted, untended, unloved by anyone, is worth—to me at least—several acres of the most assiduous cultivation.

By way of example, the haste with which I arrived in Australia helped me to understand just what I saw, and felt, and embraced in wilderness. I had left London's Heathrow, eaten chicken with doll's-house implements over the grandeur of the Alps, landed at Dhahran to find it was hot, at Dubai to find it yet hotter, at Delhi, at Kuala Lumpur in the dark and finally, a day more or less after leaving, at Darwin, where I breathed the air again instead of its airborne substitute. Another plane, a smaller one (more chicken but less altitude) and then more air at what they call the Alice. A wash-basin, a brief encounter with a busy bar, a bed, and it was soon the hour for a still smaller plane. This time the air came in at the doors, the chicken was in sandwiches, the altitude was much, much less, the pilot had to shout, and the world looked better with every mile. We landed at a spot named Giles, waited for a Toyota truck, declined the meal they offered (where do all these chickens come from?) and, driven by a momentum of impatience, I borrowed that machine and set off to savour the place.

They said something about it being wet. They said the axe was in the sack. And they shouted about the road, and spinifex, and shovels until I drove off and immediately felt content with this planet and all its works. The dust puffed from the wheels. The sun was directly overhead. I looked at my watch: 7.30, whatever that meant. I passed a tree full of—ye gods—budgerigars. I was shrieked at by a cockatoo. I shrieked back and drove faster. The mulga trees flicked by, dry-looking and none too tall for trees, but I had not expected even semi-trees in something called a semi-desert. And then there was an Aborigine, quite suddenly and on

12

his own in the mallee save for a circle of flies about his eyes. I waved but he did not wave back. He did not even look as the thing of dust and noise went by.

I sped on. The mulgas yielded to spinifex, the sharp-spined tussocks that shoot luxuriantly from soil the sun has burned to sand. It flicked at the wheels and at the axles, for it grew both in the middle and at the track's very edge. I drove even faster, intoxicated with mere air, with the sight of the sky, the smell of the earth and the total enjoyment of somewhere new. What further pleasure lay along this road? What would be round the very next bend? More budgerigars, not clawing their way from the mirror to the seed bowl, but leaping in flocks, twisting and turning in gorgeous unison? There are 4 million of these birds in Britain and none of them, alas, can fly as they did that day.

Three hours later I looked at my watch once more. To do so I had to scrape mud from its face. It said 10.30 and told me how long I had been with a very stationary machine. Around the next bend there may well have been budgerigars but there was certainly water. Like a shelving jetty the track just disappeared, apparently for ever. Much of the countryside was similarly submerged. The mulga trees were standing with their gnarled trunks in water no less stoically than others had stood in hot, dry sand a moment earlier. Plainly I only half understood the oddities of a semi-desert but I wholly comprehended, on coming round that bend, that there was dry land to the right of me and water everywhere else. It was almost with a feeling of achievement that we came to rest, the truck and I, at roughly the angle at which we had cornered so very suddenly.

Huge relief and considerable irritation are the immediate reactions to such a mishap, but, within seconds, the task ahead begins to dominate. I wondered if there were shovels on board. Ah, yes. And some sacks to put beneath the wheels or lie on during excavation. And an axe to chop down branches and provide a firmer base than mud for each deeply buried wheel.

Tunnelling from beneath the tail-board, up past the rear axle to a vantage point somewhere beneath the driver's seat, meant becoming dirty, and very hot, and not a little exhausted. What

13

gentler relaxation, therefore, than searching for one's watch along an earthy arm? Once found, there was the added puzzle of wondering what on earth, or where on earth, it meant by 10.30. I had sallied forth from Giles three hours earlier; but what of elsewhere, such as Heathrow to whose time my watch had been loyal? I lay there, front uppermost in the dirt, licking off sweat, blinking the flies away, and slowly did the sum. Australia was ten hours to the east of Greenwich. It was summer time in Britain and the clocks had been put forward. The plane had taken off at 2 p.m. and had flown through only one night. There had been one more night in the hotel, but Australia was *ahead* of Britain. Good grief, I said, on concluding the arithmetic, because less than forty-eight hours had elapsed since discovering the plane at London and finding myself in this particular predicament. I sat up, hit my head upon an exhaust bracket and laughed out loud at the nonsense of it all.

However, it was precisely what I had desired. There was no joy in shovelling red mud beneath the metallic underbelly of a station-wagon, particularly in circumstances that a mole would find cramped—at least none I could detect; but there was considerable satisfaction in the situation itself. As I laughed at my idiocy, dug into the earth, sunk the axe into a tree, hit muddily at the flies, made a foundation for the wheels to grip upon, and then sat in the seat again, I felt a kind of peace that much of life does not provide. After starting the engine and choosing reverse gear it was almost disappointing when the wheels bit sufficiently to take me back on to the road. Later, I lay in an undisturbed part of that semi-desert lake. The sky was then less blue, less hot, but redder and softer as the sun went down. The white bark of the ghost gums looked unreal, for white is always rare, and rarer still in the red heart of the southern continent; but who can query reality when the tree above his muddy head is a-chatter and a-flutter with that beloved British bird, the bulging-breasted budgie?

Later still, cleaner, invigorated, but with a very muddy machine, I met the inevitable questions.

'Glad you took the axe? And the shovel and the sacks? About three miles was it?'

'Yes.'

'What, three miles deep?'

They were a meteorological crew. They did not like their wilderness but worked there, as they said more than once, for the extra money. Even when the stars came out that evening, with the huge swathe of the southern Milky Way cutting across the sky, and one lone dingo giving voice into that night, it was still no occasion to say how much I had enjoyed becoming so closely involved with all their mud. I was about to, thinking it worth a try, and having considered a means of doing so, but someone said 'Bloody dingo,' and the moment faded away.

That day in Australia, and the speed with which its events came to pass so soon after leaving London, help to introduce this book. I was on a world wilderness tour, no less, and Australia was just one part of it. The primary reason was to make a series of television programmes, each detailing a particular kind of wilderness. The second purpose, more personal than the first, was to educate myself on the subject and pass on criteria that I might learn. After all, most of the world is wilderness—a surprising fact, particularly to those of us squeezed into conurbations—and it seemed wrong to be so ignorant about the major part of this, our planet.

A world wilderness tour! That meant attempting to find the planet as it used to be, steering clear of all development, reaching the spots where nature is pre-eminent and where the influence of man is marginal at most. It meant difficult travel. It also meant much time. I was not off just to encounter communities called foreign for their slanting eyes, or darker skins, or different styles of speech. I was off to see, insofar as this was still possible, what all their forefathers had regarded as the natural way of things, the jungle, the open plains, the untamed emptiness. I would go backwards in time rather than forwards, partly for the feeling that people have progressed sufficiently, partly I suppose for nostalgia, but mainly for that insatiable attribute called curiosity. A wilderness tour! What a pearl to fall into one's lap.

Initial planning was nothing but euphoria. I, and others, opened maps and spun a globe. It was all there waiting for us. Do not forget Antarctica, we said, or the Arctic, or the deserts, or the great mountains, or the tundra and taiga, wherever they are. And of course there is forest, dry forest, rain forest, equatorial forest; our fingers ran vaguely over the colossal Amazon. There is inland lake, and swamp, and savannah, and miles and miles of pampas, and much of it, or most of it, or all of it, was surely wilderness.

We suddenly saw the planet much as a Martian might see it. He would take note of man and all his works but then look elsewhere. He would wonder about the ice-caps at the poles and would try to think of solid snow a mile deep or more as in Antarctica. He would look at the zones next to all that ice and wonder how life can fare when plant growth is only possible for six weeks in every year. Above all, he would realise that human beings have concentrated themselves wherever agriculture has been possible and that area, more or less, is only 12 per cent of the land surface. The rest is too dry, too high, too bereft of soil, too full of rock, too wet. He would report back, possibly to the amazement of his fellows, and also to the astonishment of many humans squeezed into their city homes, that most of the planet Earth is still a wilderness.

Certainly the facts astonished me. I had seen a desert or two in my time, having travelled more than most in such emptiness, but had never added up their areas. In the northern hemisphere the desert total is 5 million square miles, about half of which is the Sahara. In the southern hemisphere, with less land at its disposal, there are 2 million square miles, half being in Australia. These enormous zones add up to 12 per cent of the land surface, or as much as man manages to use for all his crops. Of course the Martian would record this fact. He would also report that ice permanently covers 11 per cent, and mountains 9 per cent, and tundra which is too cold and too waterlogged for real growth a further 9 per cent. If semi-desert is added, the immediate total quite unfit for agriculture—and wholly fit for wilderness—is 45 per cent.

Those are the major areas, the excesses of nature. There are also the minor regions adding to this quantity. Ten per cent of Spain is bare rock, without pretension to a dusty film of soil. There are marshes that will not be drained and steepnesses that form no part of any mountain range. A single peak like Tanzania's Kilimanjaro is a pimple on the map, but its circular base is 45 miles across and therefore the area consumed by this one volcano is 1,600 square miles. It too is a wilderness set above the farmland crowded round its foot. All in all, taking infertility and frost traps, outcrops and other hindrances into account, the amount of land unlikely to be of cultivable consequence is 70 per cent of the total. The Martian would be impressed. So, as I dug out these facts, was I.

Of the remaining 30 per cent potentially suitable for agriculture the majority is still unused. The new roads of Brazil are opening up the second *half* of that country. Much of Africa is undeveloped; much of Australia; much of many crowded countries that have not yet had the political stability or the wealth to consume their emptiness. Not everywhere has been subjected to mankind for a similar length of time. No one knows when the invaders first stood on the eastern side of the Bering Strait but it is known that 16,245,000 square miles lay ahead of them, entirely without rival people, wholly for their taking. It was a new piece of land the size of Asia. Had the visitor from Mars arrived in those earlier days he would have seen everybody living in the old world and not a soul in the Americas. Even today only 11 per cent of this planet's population lives on that vast New World.

Therefore the extraterrestrial visitor would, in reporting back, be quite correct in stating that, for one reason or another, most of the planet Earth is unsuitable for the direct needs of its Earthmen. Not only is the majority of its land unusable but the great bulk of the planet is not even land of any kind. Adding the oceans and the land together, just 9 per cent of the planet's surface could be cultivated and, of that proportion, only a third is being tilled, a mere 3 per cent of the 196,950,000 square miles that is Earth's total surface area. The Martian's stay-at-home companions would therefore gain the picture of a wild world, scarcely touched by its inhabitants and impossible to use for its major part. Can this possibly be the place where we pile people into apartment blocks, burrow tunnels for their transportation and despair of finding food for every one of them?

So far, I had gone no further than the atlases, but the surprises had been considerable. Antarctica *is* 5,500,000 square miles and does double its size every winter when the surrounding sea freezes over. Australia *is* two-thirds the size of Europe, with less than 3 per cent of her numbers, but even crowded Europe possesses wilderness within its 4,000,000 square miles. There are far fewer Africans than there are Europeans and Africa is three times the size. Canada is the second largest country in the world and has half the population of Britain. Even so, its people are extraordinarily compressed. The country itself stretches from latitude 42° North up to 83° North, but every city that non-Canadians know about—Vancouver, Winnipeg, Toronto, Ottawa, Montreal, Quebec—exists within 100 miles of the American border. Great scope, therefore, for wilderness in that one land. I personally have always found it difficult to study a map unless I am off to that area or some other compelling reason exists for its perusal. Consequently, as I spun the globe in search of wilderness, I was seeing things, facts, regions, explanations I had never seen before. I was to visit the wilderness and the whole planet was at my fingertips.

Practicality then crept in. How were we to get everywhere for the filming? And when? The planet revolves and it has seasons. It is impossible to sail to Antarctica between April and November. The Arctic is similar but contrary; the ice does not even melt in the sub-Arctic Hudson Bay until mid-July. And there is darkness— total for much of each polar year. The Himalayas are best for flowers from May to August, a period also notorious for leeches, rain, cloud and a general invisibility of the great peaks. Go in winter, see the peaks, but wonder where the flowers have gone. The Amazon's rain—clogged roads, flooded airstrips—falls from November to April south of the equator. Africa's rain—well, that makes its own rules and revises them each year. I once planned a motor-bicycle trip from Capetown to Cairo. Determined not to suffer cold, rain or mud in that hot, dry, dusty continent, I studied the monthly tables carefully. If I hurried here, and dallied there, I would—or so the charts informed me—not see the vestige of a puddle for all 6,000 miles. They were right: puddle was never the word to come to mind when the land became a sea. At times, with eyes closed and body quaking, I would gasp for air as my poor pulverised brain presumed I must have sunk beneath the waves. It had been an exceptional year, they said. They always say that. I have never been to any place at any time where it has not been an exceptional year; but, in Africa, they scarcely bother to say it any more.

Gradually a world wilderness itinerary began to make sense. Between the darkness and the floods and the searing heat it proved possible to formulate a route taking account of each such variable. It meant subjecting oneself to savage change, leaving a pole for the equator, consuming anti-malarial drugs where no mosquito had ever been, and wondering absent-mindedly if the stewardess had said it was 15° or 115° outside the aircraft doors. (It was both one day.)

'What are they?' said the Mexican official, pointing to well wrapped things the shape of small grenades.

'Penguin eggs, huevos de pingüino,' I said, and so they were, but I hurried on as he choked and went off to tell his friends.

Pack mutluks with swimming gear; crampons with T-shirts; insect repellent with city suits; a hat for all seasons. Become lavishly inoculated; and documented; and authenticated. Visitors to the Falkland Islands need a White Card from Argentina. It must be requested in Argentina and cannot be issued for at least three working days. Therefore fret in Buenos Aires. Even to walk in Nepal demands a trekking permit, stating when and where the walk will take place. Humorists are alive and well in the Soviet Union. An application to visit the undoubted wilderness around Verkhoyansk was returned with a permit for some zoo not far from Moscow. I am less certain about humorists in China, but I do know they waste less time upon replies.

There was also the problem of our time. How long to spend in a place? How slowly to pass through it? Puck girdled the earth in forty minutes but, for all the information he communicated, he might as well have stayed at home. To fly by air is to experience nothing of the world beneath. I do not believe ordinary passengers can take sensible note of land flowing effortlessly six miles below, any more than they can appreciate a speed of 600 miles an hour, a temperature of minus 45°F or a pressure only 25 per cent of that at sea level. For one thing the external conditions are all lethal.

Reality consists of internal food, unctuous stewards and inane movies. It would need a crash, which everyone survived, to make the travellers understand one particle of the enormous world over which they had been flying. Then, as they progressed through the first ten yards of rain forest, they would start to absorb true facts about the wild distances still left on Earth.

Somehow I needed to crash into all such environments. Even then, imagination would be necessary to absorb their emptiness, or rather their fullness of things that have nothing to do with man. So much of our time is spent within houses, within sight of houses, or within easy reach of houses, that the comprehension of a region without any houses for hundreds of miles is difficult to achieve. The thought of actually journeying through that terrain, preferably on foot, can begin to reveal its true proportion. Geoffrey Moorhouse, wishing to be first to travel from west to east across the Sahara, studied map after map. Only when the journey was imminent did the desert materialise correctly. He saw it from an aeroplane, with eyes suddenly unscaled. 'It was the first time that the terrible immensity of that wilderness registered on my emotions rather than my intelligence. Three million square miles at once became a staggering reality, instead of a statistic paraded before the bored glance of a mathematical ignoramus.' It is always hard contemplating anything expressed in millions. What is a million square miles to the man who digs an acre? It is eleven times the size of Britain; but what is that except the exchange of one incomprehensibility for another? Everything becomes a little simpler, and truly frightening, when the distances involved have to be traversed by a pair of human feet. And no feet evoke more sympathy than one's own.

Time and again I would make errors showing I could not absorb the size of a place such as Antarctica.

'But why don't we fly here?' I would say, indicating both a fair-sized plane and a modest line on the small-scale map.

'Because that is the distance', came the chilling reply, 'from London to Chicago, and all flights here must take sufficient fuel for a return journey in case of bad weather at the destination.'

I could be equally simple about walking over lava, or through swamp, or in heat, or in extreme cold like minus 100°F, and would have to be brutally informed that corneas freeze over, bodies stiffen and ordinary Antarctic clothing is quite inadequate in such a temperature. Climbers at the top of Everest, for example, can be in conditions about 100° warmer. I found it easy to be naive when confronted by such a wealth of novelty.

This, in effect, was the setting for my secondary purpose. If wildernesses are so irrelevant to our lives, in that we neither know where they are nor comprehend their size—and half a chapter is used to make this point—what relevance do they have? The films, and the primary reason for all the voyaging, would be relatively straightforward. I would assist the camera to feast upon the beauties, strangenesses and telling points of each new area. If it was hot then I, as narrator and subject, would be hot and look hot and show, in whatever manner came best to mind, how heat can mould a place. However, the secondary reason was nothing like so simple. What point was there in wilderness?

In all history less than 30,000 men, and fewer than 100 women (most of these being Russian mariners), have ever stood on the rock and snow of Antarctica. Not a single human has ever been born there. There is no home there in the ordinary sense of that word. The majority of visitors, from the earliest sealers to today's scientists, arrive for the summer weeks. A minority actually spend a winter there and a yet smaller number pass two years on that enormous continent; but no one stays. I suspect there are more people airborne at this moment than have ever been to Antarctica, more people in a small town. Certainly more humans are added to the planet's population every five hours. So what of such a place? In mere numbers, or in weight (if that is the word) of human activity, it is negligible. At less than a thousand visitors a year it is not contributing much to human experience. At least we can all see the moon (with its even lower attendance ratings), but what are we to Antarctica and what is it to us?

It was this question, explicit for the southern wilderness but implicit for every other kind, that would accompany me around the globe. Did it all matter? What profit was there for the human spirit? Of what consequence could it be that something called tundra sits flatly and damply (for nowhere has fewer contours or more lakes) on 5 million square miles of our land. It is bigger than Europe or the United States but few of us could write as much as a paragraph about its properties; yet it lives in its fashion, a part of the planet but not a part, or so it would appear, of us. I am not suggesting it should go away, or be paved over, but I am questioning much of the current affectation which has suddenly arisen in the name of ecology, environment and wilderness.

Henry Thoreau, who is much quoted for his foresight, wisdom and terse phraseology, wrote during the early part of the last century that 'In wildness is the preservation of the world'. Perhaps that sentence is quoted most of all, for it is compact, and clear, and somewhat clever. But is it also meaningless? In political maturity (it might be argued) is the preservation of the world; or in the suppression of aggression, or in sound global government. But wildness? And what is wildness if not wilderness? A few million square miles of tundra, permafrost beneath, mosquitos above at the best of times and a total cessation of growth at every other time—the preservation of the world? Thoreau wrote practically everything he had to say in the gentle glades and lush woods near Concord, Massachusetts. Would he have changed his tune, now such a popular chant, if he had faced the katabatic winds that hit an ice shelf, the biting insect armies of central Brazil, or the kind of heat that almost killed Moorhouse as he learned the hard way just what a desert means?

I believe it is wrong to talk about wilderness when surrounded by an Eden. If the word means anything beyond a natural state of affairs, it describes a less inviting spot, the very opposite of one with milk and honey. Man may feel he is ubiquitous, for he has trespassed almost everywhere, and has even put his prints upon the moon; but mankind lives, more or less, in the spots it favours most. At least 99 per cent of us spend the great bulk of our time on or very near to agricultural soil. The wilderness is out there, beyond, far away. It is the bundu, the outback, the bush, the barren lands. It is not a place to settle and call home.

22

Therefore what should we make of it? And how will this primal wildness preserve us, as Thoreau said it would? My intial globe-spinning euphoria gave way to bewilderment. How best to see wilderness, to explore where explorers have already been? And how to live in it when even the people of each wilderness, the black Aborigines in their red world, or the raw meat eaters, as the Indians called the Eskimos, now collect their welfare cheques and live no more as their fathers used to do. To accept modern times, fly in, drive about, walk here, there and then fly out again, is likely to give as much feeling of a wilderness as a stroll through a botanical hot-house will give of the mighty Amazon. Instead I would just have to use every opportunity that came my way, walk and stumble and peer and grab at every offering. I would record as much as I could, the facts, the feelings, the fringe items that are fun at the time or quaint in retrospect. I would look up the history, discover anecdotes, experience climate and steep myself in the arrogant humility of the questioning newcomer. I would see and feel and heed the wilderness.

The globe spun beneath a fingertip. It was high time I moved on to the real thing. I spun it more, then stopped it suddenly. It came to rest with my finger pointing firmly at a spot of ocean somewhere to the north of Antarctica.

2 *Ice*

And yet I think there must be some [land] to the South behind
this ice; but if there is, it can afford no better retreat for birds,
or any other animals, than the ice itself.
James Cook (January 1774)

The ship was bucking south through the waters of the Drake
Passage. The latitude was 60°S, the longitude 60°W and the sea
outside looked much as it can look almost anywhere, cold, unwelcoming and very alien; but the birds were different. There were
Wilson's petrels skimming at the foaming water-line. There were
giant petrels, flying the same wind with less energy but apparently
more skill, and occasionally swooping below wave height much as
fulmars often do. And then, quite alone even in this crowd, there
were albatrosses, relaxed perfectionists at flight. The light too was
different. The season was early December, towards the peak of
midsummer, and the sun was taking its time to travel down the
sky. Each hour seemed to last for the length of two as the day went

---

Antarctica is breathtakingly beautiful, daunting, dangerous. It is the coldest,
highest, windiest continent, but no one even saw it until 1820 or wintered there
until 1898. Right, near Port Lockroy at 64°S. Overleaf, Adélie penguins, Elephant
seals and a Husky.

24

on and on. The sun hung there, and time hung there, and stomach and rhythms followed suit for neither appetite nor sleepiness emerged to break the day.

A notice had been pinned in the recreation room. It welcomed everybody to bet upon the exact time that those on watch in the wheel-house 'would first sight a berg or bergy bit'. Like the *Titanic*'s captain I smirked gently but put down a random hour before going outside to have a look. Certainly it was cold, but crossing from Dover to Calais can be cool, and no bits of bergs appear to confuse those straits. I watched the petrels, gazed at that timeless sun, saw nothing in the water but occasional streaks of kelp, and then hurried back to the firmer reality of darts, noise, drink and argument. I had forgotten about supper, and was happily forgetting about sleep, as there seemed no need, when someone shouted and everyone rushed to the side. Or almost everyone, because I still could not credit the sudden appearance of blocks of ice. Eventually I peered, but it had been a long drinking evening, twelve hours or more, and the room's window was unclean, being flecked with spray, and I could see nothing of any berg. The rest rushed to the notice and poured money into one man's hands before I turned up my collar to go outside. As I gazed, craning forward to cut down the distance by half a foot or so, it did begin to seem as if a blob were there. I climbed up three decks to have a better look and the blob grew firmer as my reward. Presumably there were still petrels, and foam on the waves, and assuredly the sun still shone, but now I saw only that bergy lump a dozen miles away. The air had become, quite dramatically, unbelievably cold (we had crossed the Antarctic Convergence, where cold southern air savagely meets the relative warmth of air from elsewhere), and the white thing drew nearer and vastly bigger. Just how big was it? How tall and how long?

Melting icebergs are not only bright with colour but they crack noisily as bubbles of compressed air are released. Only seventeen species of bird nest on the Antarctic mainland. Left, a Dominican gull and, right, a Giant petrel.

Wilderness

'Oh, it's a baby. Half a mile; no more,' they said in the wheel-house, and I rushed outside again.

At that size, however babyish, it was the biggest single moving thing I had ever seen. It was about fifty feet high, which meant, give or take quite a bit, some two or three hundred feet below the surface. The proportion varies considerably because a freshwater iceberg (made originally from snow) is lighter than a saltwater berg (made, of course, from frozen sea) and therefore sits higher in the water, but both kinds float less deeply if the water supporting them is salt rather than fresh, or if a lot of air has been trapped inside their shapes. My mind congealed at these thoughts, but I estimated the breadth and depth of that half-mile thing, multiplied them together, and then turned it all into weight. The baby, moving solely on its own and now three miles away, tipped the scales at 17 million tons. Even an Egyptian pyramid does not weigh that much. Faced by this fact and the numbing cold I lumbered indoors again.

'Do you believe in it now?' they said.

'Not entirely.'

The next day we moved into a whole new planet. The phrase came to mind then and has never left me. It was a place on earth the like of which I had never seen before. The night had not been a good one, with thumping engines, continual sunlight, a bunk not big enough, the ebullience of those who rise early, and an acute internal misunderstanding about the total lack of food; but the morning was, as I have said, beyond this world.

The shape of Antactica is like that of a flea. Most of it is a hunched and rounded carapace but jutting north is an angular limb they call the peninsula. They also call it Graham Land, and Palmer Land, and Tierra de San Martin and O'Higgins Land, for different countries have had differing ideas, but everyone who has been there is agreed that the western side of this peninsula is a splendid confusion of some of the most striking scenery in all the continent.

Anyone going there for the first time just blinks and stares at it. To sail down the Lemaire Channel, as we were doing, and to head for Port Lockroy, is to be privileged beyond all doubt. Where to look first? The sky has a clarity never seen before; it makes opaque all other memories. They say you can see for 150 miles on such clear days, but I would have believed ten times more because the air was quite invisible. Just what was it that I had been looking through earlier in life? A fuzz, a haze, and a mistiness that had suddenly gone away.

The land itself was white, and brightly so. It stood high on either side of us, 3,000 feet or more, and only occasionally did sharp streaks of rock jut through to give point to that endlessness of white. There were white walls, where a piece had broken off, and white ribs where crevasses had been formed. And all of this— the peaks, the great buttresses, the walls and falls of snow—was duplicated in the water as if a single wonder was simply not enough. The reflections were just as perfect, for there was not a breath of wind, no ripple, no wavering of that excellence above the water-line.

Within the sea itself, apart from the mirror image of the land, were tens of thousands of fragments of floating ice, smooth bits, flat bits, sculptured bits and broken bits. Nothing else, not even the land itself, can fashion itself into such a variety of form, for there were straight lines, complete circles, triangles and all the mishmash of every other shape between such regularities. The language tries to follow suit, for there is talk, of course, of snow and ice and bergs and bergy bits, but also of pack, pancake, loose pack, fast pack, sastrugi and frazil, piedmont and shelf, growlers and blink and brash and grease. To the uninitiated, unfamiliar with the accepted terms, there are cathedrals and tables, Henry Moores and Barbara Hepworths, husks and hulks, all askew and turned on end, each with a magic worth a stare.

They were coloured too, mainly blue, but often green, and sometimes with a great streak of orange where some plankton, I presume, had been frozen into place. Straight on, or where the sun struck most blindingly, they were always white. The blues and greens were at their best in the thin parts, or down at the water's edge. And at that edge, where the warmer sea had eaten into the ice, there was a tapering of the shape, a groove, a weakening. In time this would be sufficient to turn the whole thing upside-down, or partly so, merely making it shift its stand like a table missing some legs. The old water-line would then be at a new angle, and so would the one before it, while the sea would begin again to etch its mark upon the berg.

Quite apart from the enormous variety of form, I had not expected to see icicles upon what, in former times, they called ice islands; but when the wind freshens to move the sea it lifts and drops the bergs that sit on it. They are dunked, and raised and dunked again, and gradually a grille of icicles is formed. These too can be coloured and they add to all the oddnesses of shape when the whole thing tilts making their jagged line lie at some other angle to the sea. Over 4,000 shapes of snowflake have allegedly been photographed, but such a task would be infinite for all the kinds of berg and bergy bit.

Then we met animals. Two whales surfaced, blew, and quickly sank again. They were the first I had ever seen. What a miserable state of affairs! I have travelled a lot, and been on water quite a lot, and yet I had to reach 65 °S before seeing a fellow mammal whose dominion used to be the seven seas. The Lemaire Channel had been particularly rich in whales; yet here were two, just two. They surfaced again, blew, arched over irritatingly before giving us a proper sight, and then submerged once more. A great piece of pack was ahead of them, a flat shape made occasionally jagged by bergs frozen into it, and beneath this they vanished. Each year 37,000 large whales are killed, mostly in Antarctic waters, their final refuge, and we had seen just two.

There were also penguins. To begin with I thought them to be porpoises, a ludicrous error; but there was a leaping, a diving and a speed that made more sense for porpoises than for any kind of bird. Moreover, their small, black backs were arched and, when travelling rapidly from a fast intruding ship, they bore no relation to the waddling, dinner-jacketed comedians who more often come our way. Once again I found myself resenting the speed of events. The leaps were too fast, and the dives too momentary. Even with a shoal (or is it a flock?) the action is too brief to comprehend.

I do not know why one piece of pack should have been so favoured, but a leopard seal had chosen to clamber on to it. Sleek, dappled and as innocent as a languid snake it lay there, basking in the cold and on the ice. I have no idea if it was hungry but I could see that a leaping, diving, skimming penguin group had that same piece of pack in mind. The ice, with its invisible inhabitant, had been singled out as a suitable resting spot and the birds leaped towards it, leap-frogging through the waves. The seal just lay there, unaware of the food speeding on its way. The food, equally ignorant of its danger, busily shortened both distance and odds. I, and others, gazed aghast.

Penguins of all kinds make a landfall much as a missile leaves a submarine. They rise upright from the water with such momentum that they have nothing more to do than wait for the land or the ice to be beneath their feet. Then a step or two, if need be, to regain posture and they change in an instant from porpoises into the birds we know. They also change, if there happens to be a leopard seal upon the ice, from an orderly group into a frantic turmoil of dithering uncertainty. More and more were leaping from the water only to add to the tremulous anxiety of those already there. The birds did not leap back again—and for a reason. Most penguins meet their deaths in the water: that is where the seal and killer whale can strike effectively, and land of any kind is a haven by comparison. Instinct dictates a longing for land when danger is around as there are no predators on land for any adult birds—at least, there should not be. Out of water the seal is a scarcely mobile slug. In it the animal is swift as an arrow, barbed with teeth, and death for those who cannot escape. To swim might be lethal. To stand, whatever the view, was undoubtedly the wiser course; but mere wisdom can often seem inappropriate.

The birds jostled, looked with each eye in turn, shuffled, moved further to the rear, stumbled, and picked themselves up almost before they fell. The seal, it must be admitted, did nothing but lie there. The birds supplied the action. They plainly grew more desperate each moment, each second, and the situation could not last. One of them, half pushed by the others but half inclined that way, fell into the water. Then, as if his companions were linked in one long chain, they were inexorably drawn to the take-off point and there fell overboard. The chain gathered haste and the final dozen vanished almost simultaneously, leaving the seal precisely as it had been before the precipitate invasion. The invaders, making all speed and no longer in a flock, were a scattering of little rounded backs smoothly putting distance between themselves and that perilous piece of pack.

They had been Adélies, the most common penguin of Antarctica. Later, to round off this particular story, I met them on land. The desire to do so was very strong and I snatched the first opportunity that came my way. The day was just as perfect, blue, bright, windless, and I strode happily to an Adélie rookery further up the slope. Some noise, more expostulation than anything else, indicated a disturbance at the site. Full of protest and clamour, it lasted a while before a group of penguins disentangled themselves from their fellows and set off down the hill.

I stopped at the noise. There was so much to see and, plainly, events were coming my way. Initially came one of those realisations that strike so suddenly: penguins have difficulty in walking over snow. They move down an icy slope with as much apparent confidence and skill as, say, an armadillo negotiating rocks. They slip, slither, slide, stop, fall, toboggan, and only gradually proceed. I had imagined the ritual might be performed with rather more grace, but could not have been more enchanted with the actual scene. Besides, the group was still coming straight towards me. Most creatures, as we know too well, give a wide berth to humans in their path. Not so these penguins; they walked and waddled as if it was a normal day without a beacon of a figure standing in their path. To stand tall on white snow, decked in the bright blues and reds of Antarctic clothing, surrounded by that non-existent air and lit by a sun of extraordinary brilliance, is to be wildly conspicuous. It is to be like the soldier who turns left, not right, or the dancer who falls down.

Nevertheless, the penguins marched on. They must have noticed the great pink-faced statue standing before them, but gave no sign of doing so. At least it was not a leopard seal, however different it might be from anything they had ever seen before. So they occupied themselves with the tortuous business of progress,

30

paddling with their wings and then standing or falling again according to the slope. Steadily they reduced the gap between man and bird. They staggered; I stood. They failed to take account of me; I noticed nothing else but them. Eventually their group was all about me and, as chance would have it, one individual progressed straight for my left boot and fell straight over it. There was a sharp grunt of protest as a beak jabbed into the snow. There was then a blink and look of protest as the bird struggled to its feet. There was finally a peck, a fairly savage peck, at the boot so blatantly to blame. With that done, this offended creature rejoined the others and soon leapt into the freezing sea.

No one could possibly forget the first experience with such a bird. To have been a French explorer's wife a century and a half ago may have been a lonely business, and I know nothing about the lady called Adélie d'Urville, wife of Dumont. But to have your name grafted on such a piece of creation as the commonest penguin of Antarctica must, if immortality attracts you, be a gorgeous way of finding it.

The first day's sailing in the Lemaire Channel, the dropping of our anchor at Port Lockroy (no port, just a name and great beauty dipping down into the sea), the first hours on land and the very first encounter with a penguin rookery were a series of astonishments. Although the feeling of amazement might have waned a little as time went by, it did nothing of the sort. Each day brought new discoveries. In a way that first day never really ended. There were meals, and I would crawl into my bunk from time to time, but in fact the sun never set because it was midsummer and soon we were south of the Antarctic circle. There was always daylight and therefore a physical unwillingness to think of sleep just because external time-pieces had ticked a day away. It was one's own internal clock, the normal watch-dog of one's life, that had gone awry.

The ship I sailed on was the R.R.S. *Bransfield*. Her annual task was to leave England around October fully laden with supplies, stop off at the Falkland Islands to pick up people and more things, and then travel round the British bases in Antarctica, delivering recruits, recovering old hands and off-loading the necessities of

Wilderness

life—food, drink, fuel, equipment, building materials. Antarctica can supply nothing but air, rock (and that not everywhere), ice and snow. Each base has to have a year's supply of goods over and above its normal needs—just in case the relief ship cannot reach it. Each year is different—more ice, less ice, more wind (and more about that later), or just a trail of circumstances that can stop a ship from reaching every place along the line.

I, along with some scientists destined for a two-year stay, had arrived at Stanley in the Falklands to await the ship steaming from the north. To reach Stanley it is necessary to spend bureaucratic time in Buenos Aires, not that this is harsh as impositions go, before heading for the Aeroparque with a ticket for Comodoro Rivadavia. Time there could be tedious. I spent a day searching for its charms, saw shanty slums, many sad Indian eyes, a lot of concrete and nothing that made me wish to miss the once-weekly Argentine air force plane. The Falklands, when they loomed, were large, numerous and not mere specks as famous islands often are. Our wheels bit into an airstrip more gravelly than most and suddenly, after days of travel, I was apparently back where I had started from.

The place had an Englishness even England would find hard to emulate. 'Arrivals' was a Nissen hut. There was a policeman, helmeted traditionally, and the kind of banter that the English do, if not well, at least consistently. At the Upland Goose hotel, the largest place in town, I could not believe I was 6,000 miles from home. The lavatory clanked, wheezed, whined and had to be jerked to liberate its brief gush, and the handle, and the bowl, and the door's ineffectual lock were all as British as the quasi-helpful notices sprinkled here and there. I went to open the modest window, fiddled with its catch, withdrew a folded Player's cigarette packet, and abruptly caught both rows of fingers when the top half of that window-pane thumped its message home to me. Of course the sash-cord would have gone. I laughed and fell upon the bed and it twanged as they do in Skegness, and I laughed again when, to keep me company, the wardrobe door gaped open to creak its own distinctive tune. The lamb that evening was lovely and so were the greengages and custard.

32

The Falklands are on the same latitude as the English Midlands but have the feel and look of the Orkneys. The winds can be terrific and, instead of double glazing or any such fancy notions to counter the cold, there are pubs galore and you struggle through the gale to reach their warming sanctuary. The drink is cheap, I think, but everyone behaves as if some whisky-laden galleon has come to grief upon the shore. Which, for all I know from those raucous evenings, may well have been the case.

The *Bransfield* arrived on schedule to rescue us. The launch trip, with water whipping straight from the waves and a wind still roaring directly from the Horn, did wonders and we were whole again, even if wet and cold and out of breath, as we climbed aboard. We steamed south that night and two days later met that staggering berg afloat on the same high seas. One more day, after the magic of Lemaire, and we arrived at the first of the British bases to off-load supplies, drop people, hand over mail and, of course, go ashore.

It is frequently accepted, certainly by the Americans and even by some others, that the first person ever to see the Antarctic mainland was a young man from Connecticut named Nathaniel B. Palmer. Aged 20, he was captain of the 30-foot (some say 45-foot, which seems more reasonable) sloop *Hero* out from Stonington in company with four other vessels in search of fur seals. The flotilla's leader had suggested that Palmer should head further south and, in that year of 1820, he saw high mountains on what is now known to have been the mainland. A piece of the earth, as big as the United States and Mexico together and forming 26 per cent of all land south of the equator, had managed to hide itself until that moment. Captain Cook and others had searched for Terra Australias, alleged to exist on no authoritative grounds whatsoever, and had probed south into regions of frost-smoke and ice-islands, but then they had yielded to the call of Tahiti and of the Pacific Ocean that encompasses, after all, half the world. Therefore a modest sealer carried off the prize. (Other claimants of this same prize are the British captains William Smith and Edward Bransfield sailing in the *Williams* and the Russian captain Thaddeus Bellingshausen of the *Vostok*. Everyone is entitled to make a personal choice as extra facts are thin on the ground. My choice, as above, is Palmer.)

However, Palmer could not land owing to the ice. The continent is beautiful but not immediately welcoming to those with a hold to fill, a profit to make and a small boat powered solely by the wind. In wildness, proclaimed Thoreau from the warmth of his self-made home, is the preservation of the world. Palmer, his contemporary, dodging the bergs that towered above his boat, would have found it hard to comprehend his fellow countryman. Eventually others did land upon the continent, practical men wishing to kill, to careen a boat, to hack fresh water from the shore. It was difficult to gain a footing. The enormous quantity of snow on the continent means that its sea-edge is almost always steep, a buttress, a precipice, a thick icing to the cake.

I found it hard to grasp the concept of so much solid snow. The actual annual precipitation is very little, equivalent to two inches of rain over the bulk of Antarctica or six inches near its frontier with the sea. However, the precipitation arrives as snow. It cannot run away or make rivers. It becomes compressed and adds its mite to the weight already there. About 90 per cent of the world's ice sits on Antarctica, which represents almost 2 per cent of the Earth's supply of water (or all the rain and snow to have fallen anywhere in the past fifty years). The snow's depth is not, as we measure it in other continents, the grand total of one winter's effort, but the fallen aggregate of countless centuries. Average thickness is estimated at 7,500 feet, and depths over twice that have been recorded. That is, to say it again, more than one mile and, in parts, almost three miles deep. Consequently, Antarctica is far and away the highest continent. When Robert Scott stood at the South Pole, proclaiming it to be a dreadful place, he had over 9,000 feet of ice beneath his badly bitten toes.

Nevertheless the situation is not static, a simple accumulation of each year's increment. At all times the ice is moving. Not only is it plastic but is is elastic, containing compression and then yielding it again. In the main, of course, it moves downhill, away from the centre and towards the sea. The year has even been calculated when the bodies of Scott and his companions will each become part of a berg. The actual ice at the South Pole is now known to be moving towards Rio at between twenty-seven and thirty feet a year. At Halley Bay the British base moved three miles in the first ten years after it was built upon the ice. The sea finally accepts all offerings. If the land nearby is steep the fragments will be small, broken off piecemeal as the flat waves hit them; but, if the land slopes gently, the burden of ice may bend to float upon the sea, and an enormous shelf will project itself from the continent. When Ross sailed into the sea that bears his name he penetrated farther to the south in that area than anyone since has been able to do. An enormous lip of ice, hundreds of feet high and several hundred miles across, has pushed further and further from the land since he and his ship were first dwarfed by it.

It is thought that all the ice at present on Antarctica, even from the Pole of Inaccessibility, correctly and forbiddingly named, will have crept, flowed and, in contorted fashion, reached the sea over the next 100,000 years. It will become bergs, bergy bits, and all the rest, before moving north and finally melting out of sight. Two per cent of the world's water will then have rejoined the great majority, but another 2 per cent will have fallen upon the continent as snow.

It is from the ice-shelves that the biggest bergs are formed. The flow of ice, imperceptible and vast, is continuous. It pushes out into the sea; but the sea is a moving thing and there are storms, and one day a crack in the ice will grow sufficiently for it to become a gap. Something the size of an English county or a small American State will then be on its own. Bergs 90 miles long have been reported, some 130 feet high with another 600 feet beneath the surface. On seeing such a monster, and wondering if there is room for it to be afloat beneath the water-line, it is fun looking at the chart and noting whether there are 100 clear fathoms along its tremendous length. Naturally the true coastline is totally obscured, both for radar and for normal eyes, by such extra-ordinary ice-islands lying in between. The story is told, and readily believed, of navigators who have lost their way by mistaking the great bulk of a passing berg, or even one grounded a few hundred feet below, for the continent itself.

Wilderness

Although Antarctica was first seen in 1820, and word of it must have passed around amongst sealers and whalers despite their traditional secrecy at passing on discovery, no one thought of wintering there. When the explorers moved in and actually published what they had found there was still no rush to invade, to build, or to stay for more than weeks. The marine pickings were good—notably the fur seals and oil-rich whales—but the more new facts that were learned about this new land the more forbidding a place it seemed to be.

For one thing, it was unutterably cold. Because the Earth is 3 million miles nearer the sun in December than in June it might be expected that the southern hemisphere has colder winters, and so it does. Also, because the Antarctic ice sheet is so much greater and higher than anything in the north, it might be expected that this too exerts a chilling influence, and so it also does. The Arctic is relatively hot by comparison. In Antarctica, and near the Pole of Inaccessibility (which is also near the south magnetic pole), the thermometers have dropped to minus 126°F (or minus 88°C). Nowhere in the north is ever as cold as that.

As another hazard, it is quite the windiest continent on Earth. Sir Douglas Mawson's expedition of 1912 recorded an average windspeed of 50 mph throughout the year, 85 mph for 24 hours and 107 mph for 8 hours. Other expeditions have recorded winds of 200 mph when the cold air from the plateau above has been caused to hurtle downhill with incredible ferocity. It is the wind that kills more than the temperature. On a calm day below freezing, and if the sun is shining brightly, shining with all its might, it can be hot; but should a breeze spring up, just a whisper of movement at a mile or two an hour, it is suddenly very, very cold. One rushes for more clothes. Should the temperature actually be cold and the sky overcast (and I remember a telling day 7,000 feet up on the peninsula at 70°S) the abrupt arrival even of a moderate wind can be actually terrifying (and I also remember stumbling to a tent, with a body doubly assaulted by wind and cold).

Nevertheless, mankind will put up with extremely disagreeable conditions, and does so, when it feels it has reason—such as gold, glory or other gain. Unfortunately for those seeking gold in any form the Antarctic became less and less of a lure. Practically none of its land surface, 3 per cent at most, is ever exposed from its tomb of ice and certainly nothing instantly valuable has been found upon that fragment of its surface. There is also hardly any life, beyond the mammals and birds cavorting in or near the sea. There are no trees, no herbs, no woody shrubs, no ferns throughout that wind-blown, ice-cold continent. In time men found two flowering plants, one a pink and the other a grass, and that is all—to date. There are 70 species of moss, 350 of lichen, and, although colourful on occasion and even extensive (there is a thousand-foot slope of moss near one British base), they do not give the feeling of a bountiful, abundant Earth that can be so heart-warming. In fact, the largest creature to live entirely off the land is *Parochlus steinenii*, a fly not quite three millimetres long. It has wings but rarely uses them. A near rival in size, *Belgica antarctica*, another fly existing on the continent, is actually wingless. Plainly there is not much point in going very far by air in that freezing, windy place. A better notion is to stay put in some reasonable micro-climate, say within the moss, and exist like the springtails and mites that form the majority of visible creatures making a living on this emptiest continent.

The life that does abound is leaping and diving in the sea. There are six species of seal, seven of whale, a considerable variety of fish, and a great quantity of plankton, particularly near the Antarctic edge. Some forty species of bird have been identified, but only seventeen of these actually make their nest on the Antarctic mainland. All these birds save one have webbed feet, once again emphasising the sea's role as the crucial source of food. The single exception to webbing is the sheathbill, but even it feeds from the shore. The greatest exception among the fish in this part of the world, a part where abnormality seems entirely reasonable, is *Chaenocephalus aceratus*, the so-called ice-fish. It is the only vertebrate known to exist without any red cells in its blood. How it uses oxygen has still to be discovered.

Whatever the relative bounty of the sea, man is a terrestrial creature, and as a piece of land the Antarctic has proved modest in its ability to attract. The first man to overwinter there did so entirely by mistake. Adrien de Gerlache, of Belgium, was trapped in the ice towards the end of the southern summer of 1898. Not for twelve months was his ship released and, together with the first facts to be gathered from an Antarctic winter, he hurried north for home. With the arrival of the new century a new attitude sprang up. The daunting qualities of Antarctica that had kept it fairly free from men suddenly became a set of hurdles, no less fearful, that had to be overcome. Very little more was known about the place, and nothing more that seemed desirable, but the heroic age began. The gain now was glory, with a tinge of science to make the honour greater still. There were no obvious deeds to accomplish, few peaks to climb, but there was a pole, latitude 90° South. The accounts that Amundsen and Scott gave of this place, and the fact that five of the ten men to reach it died soon afterwards, certainly discouraged others. Consequently, not until the aeroplane had been soundly developed and a man could fly there safely did anyone else reach that southernmost spot. In 1956 Admiral George Dufek, of the US Navy, was the first to touch the place after Scott and his companions had turned from it to hurry north.

I too, having arrived safely and soundly, hurried to set foot on Antarctica as soon as opportunity permitted, 153 years after Palmer, Smith, Bransfield and Bellingshausen had first seen the place, 75 years after de Gerlache had passed a twelve month there, 62 years after Scott and Amundsen had played their parts and a mere 17 years after Dufek had stepped from a plane named *Che Sera Sera*. I hurried nonetheless. A group of us clambered down the rope ladder, leaped more or less gingerly into the scow recently winched into the water, and looked ahead at the land. In fact, it had disappeared. Low in the water, the scow was set about with all manner of bits of berg and through these, and past these, and headlong into these we noisily made our way. At times more in retreat than advance, we grunched and thumped and groped a passage to the shore.

The quayside seemed to come no nearer, with its couple of huts, many masts and one Union Jack, but the *Bransfield* grew smaller. No longer could we hear the ribaldry when a chosen waterway between the ice became a dead end as they, not we, could see. The penguins would leap from the floes as we cannoned into them, and streak briefly, but oh so fast, through the water by our bows. More scrunching and grunching (and just what shielded our propeller?) when there came further ribaldry, but this time from the quay. Ten men stood there who had not seen any other humans for almost ten months. There was a certain amount of chat, but not much. They say, for those who like the place, that the relief ship's arrival is not entirely joyful. For those who did not fare so well, who have just spent a dark winter regretting the fact of having arrived, it is easy to imagine that they too would be speechless when the day of escape arrived.

I walked ashore. The immediate impression was of smell, and mud, and junk galore. From the jetty, itself a twenty-foot piece of planking, there was a muddy causeway up to the huts which passed through walls of snow. On each side were packing cases, exposed to everything the elements could do but not to the bacteria that rot such wood for us. They looked as good as new. There were tins and jars, old hunks of machinery, concrete pipes, plastic pipes, sledge runners, tractor tracks and fuel drums; oh yes, there were plenty of those. I still worried about the smell and found it half buried in the snow. About fifty crab-eater seals were there with mouths bared, showing the beautiful and almost fan-like molars that they possess. These dead beasts were food for the dogs, howling with excitement from their staked positions in the snow at the sight of unaccustomed visitors. There must have been decay to make that smell, but not much, for such a wealth of death would have made a stench for miles around in any other place.

I went indoors. It had some of the feel, if not the space, of a ski hotel, with lots of boots, heavy clothes hanging on hooks, and people clumping by. Off the central passageway were small rooms with double bunks, more clothes, personal things, single glazing on the window frames, and a climate that, unlike a ski hotel, was rather cool. Then came a radio room, bleeping and whining on its own, and next a library—or was it the boiler room with books stored for use as fuel? Certainly there was a stove, glowing red inside, and the air was desert dry, but a host informed me that 'Fids like it hot when they've been in the mank'.

I sat down. The heat seemed hotter. I wondered how the volumes survived as some covers were almost circular.

'Is this where you curl up with a good book?' I laughed, warmly, but on my own.

'What?' he said. 'I don't get you.'

'Let's go back to what you said for I didn't get you either.'

Presumably all isolated groups acquire jargon. Days in Antarctica can be dingle, with clear skies, or mank, with nothing of the sort. Food is scradge, which is unkind I feel on the food, and people are Fids with a King Fid as their boss. Another custom is to wear your long and thick issue tartan shirt (we collected ours from Kit-a-Fid at Stanley) so that it hangs firmly outside whatever trousers you are wearing at the time.

Which brings me, abruptly and with little cause, to the subject of women. I was told before leaving that the British send 20-year-olds to Antarctica, the Americans send older men with psychiatrists, and the Russians send women along with their men, whatever their age. There is a speck of truth in this story (which is ample if the tale is good enough) but the greater truth is that this last refuge of a continent has been and still is a largely male preserve. In 1947 two ladies overwintered in an American base a few hundred yards of snow away from a British base; but, if one probes delicately ('O.K., so how did it work out?'), it is as if one were inquiring into a well-buried crime. Spencer Tracy, some may recall encountered a similar rebuff when he stopped off at Black Rock.

Nevertheless the main feeling, or rather the main feeling expressed by young and old, by the senior men and by the beginners (as with 75 per cent of the British—'Never been south of Torquay before,' said one) is that women should stay back home. Not all the Fids go on sledging journeys, a traditionally masculine occupation; some cook, man the radio or stagger no farther than the met. site. Women, even for traditionalists, could do such things and therefore, one assumes, it is their sexual capabilities that are banished from this scene. They could, it is roundly said, cause havoc. They could also, it is never said, provide a different viewpoint, be better listeners than the average male, create a more customary atmosphere (after all, one does encounter them frequently elsewhere) and add their virtues to those of a group of men.

It is apparent, whether or not any possible havoc would be effectively counterbalanced by possible benefits, that men do like situations demanding male-only company. Various requirements have been relaxed. There is no need to be a male. The very fact of being there, with the cold, the wind and the isolation, is already masculine. This may even help with recruiting. Open up Antarctica to the other half of the population and, there no longer being exclusively, it might be twice as hard to gain acceptances. At least there were no mammary ladies pinned to the walls, or none that I saw, and the talk was never changing-room talk, but people might just be right about the havoc. It must be unnerving watching the relief ship sail, knowing that nine months of days are ahead with no more company; but perhaps this very lonely test of self is one excitement of the place. I look quizzically at the only female pictures pinned upon the wall. They were all of Princess Anne.

'Why on earth her?' I said, probing gently once again.

'Don't you know? You are behind the times,' a man replied. I certainly did not know and still do not and doubtless never will.

From this hut, and more like it as the trip progressed, I and the others would sally forth, making our film, seeing the place, absorbing this new planet of a continent. Mere progress was almost always difficult, either across the snow or the water. The snow could be soft, making one wish for skis, or ice-hard, making one curse oneself for bringing skis along. The water could be clear and then, when you had safely landed, the wind could shift to fill it up with ice. There was always ice somewhere that the wind could rustle up if need be to keep us confined on board for days on end or anxiously confined on land until the wind had changed again. The shapes of all these blocks of ice were no less varied when seen from close at hand, and no less colourful, but from afar I had never dreamed they might be noisy things. They go off like firecrackers. Bubbles of air have been compressed in them and these explode at the first opportunity melting brings their way. Of course there is air with snow when it settles on the ground. That same air is frozen into place as the snow settles into ice and then, firmly trapped, the bubbles are buried and moved and fearfully compressed. Perhaps not for tens of thousands of years does that ice with its encapsulated air break off to form a berg. Even then the ice must melt before, with a snap and a crack, its air pops free again.

Every now and then were patches of bare land, with exposed rock and even small tussocks of the one kind of grass. These were the places, by and large, most favoured by the nesting birds. The Adélies, in particular, were fond of stony sites, using bits of rock to make their nests, taking more from their fellows and, in doing so, losing from behind as much as they gained in front. The scent of a rookery (only equalled, as I discovered 10,000 miles later, by walruses) is memorable and foul but made instantly agreeable by the sight of the birds themselves. Before I can be accused of having a fixation about small dinner-jacketed objects it must be admitted that everyone else seems to come under their spell despite that smell. Static they are delightful. Squabbling they are noisy, but no less disarming. On the move, as I have already said, they are an excellence. The eggs are dirty, and only an optimist would believe that such besmirched and chalky things resting on the rock could harbour life; but in December the fluffy chicks crack out to make their cheep heard in all the cackling, choking, croaking of the adults standing over them.

There were also blue-eyed cormorants that made the sky's bright blue seem pallid; Antarctic terns, chattering and diving in a manner indistinguishable from their Arctic relatives; and giant petrels, looking too big and too grand for such a humble task as sitting on an egg. They, like the penguins and even, in the main, the cormorants, would not move just because a human came their way. I do resent the fact that creatures should be so loath to have us near them that they fly away or maintain a distance, a policy they do not generally keep for other animals. Of course they, or their ancestors, have often had cause. We have killed, and caught,

42

and behaved aggressively; but not with every creature. We have also tended and loved when opportunity has arisen. I believe we might do so even more if there was not such immediate resentment, a fluttering away as though we were unclean. I am always overjoyed when, as in Antarctica, a creature does not behave as if a pariah had come its way. Each act of courage by one animal, each close acquaintanceship, will surely make it harder for us to do harm. Creatures would do better, in the main, I firmly believe, if they did not immediately insult us by flying somewhere else.

Like the elephant seals. Not that they could fly anywhere, being three tons in weight, but they could flee and fail to provide a further Antarctic delight. We came across some on a beach. It was a cool day, with a wind of about thirty knots and flurries of snow that settled in the creases of one's clothes, but the animals lay there as if it were Africa before the sun had set. I have never seen such corporal indolence. I have never seen such grossness or such abject attitudes, but then never before, outside a zoo, had I seen the elephant seal. There were twelve of them, lying alongside and athwart each other in a space more suited for eight. Their breath hung steamily about them and occasionally they would grunt, lengthily and awfully, much as a wash basin will do when, in a poorly plumbed hotel, the next room lets its water run away. As they did so some substance from within would be gargled up to drool and drip about their mouths. Of course, at this stage in the description, it might be expected that they would defecate as well, just where they lay, and so they did.

It is not wrong to say that the scene was pure joy. They were great, magnificent, fantastic animals and, to cap it all, they did not mind my proximity. I scratched a belly to be rewarded with a croak, a pigsty gush of air and more of that porridge-like saliva about the creature's mouth. It then relaxed, solid with fatigue. A dominican gull, flying uncertainly against the wind, landed heavily a few beasts down from mine, but did not even earn awareness from the steaming, bulging thing beneath its feet. I was flattered that these monsters had permitted me, briefly as it was bitter cold, to be at one with them. When I did leave them the snow was falling faster and that round dozen still lying on the shore had all but vanished beneath it.

Most days were clear, dingle not mank. We would film the creatures, be for ever amazed at the brightness of the air, sit watching icebergs and icicles and wonder, yet again, at the length of every day. With so much light (more falls here in midsummer than at the equator), and with so much snow to bounce it back again, our faces suffered frightfully. We had listened to the sages, put on unguents, worn goggles and peaked caps, but the radiation still got through. Our faces, more seared than burned, looked unwholesome, but our lips were grotesque and grew in size enormously before they cracked under the strain. I thought, on first seeing the continent, that someone had stripped away the atmosphere. I subsequently knew, on looking at a bleeding irradiated face, how right I had been. One longed for mank, not dingle, to give the wounds a chance.

One fine day in the middle of the night I experienced the extreme pleasure of driving a team of dogs. We had been on a short foray inland, during which we had learned something of polar travel: how everything fits precisely on the sledge, how the tent is raised by sticking two of its feet in the snow and then letting the wind assist you in jabbing the two front feet of the tented pyramid in the ground. Food boxes anchor the tent's material on the upwind side. The dogs are pegged down in their running order, with dog, bitch, dog alternating along the length of nine. Through the round entrance hole, always downwind, and inside the tent there is a food container and the radio box between two beds. A primus will dry all clothes hung in the tent's apex. The arrangement of food, and the procedure for cooking it, has been worked out over the years so that its finesse and economy of space is as near perfect as can be contrived.

It needs to be. The Antarctic is unforgiving about gross mistakes or even minor errors in procedure. It pounces upon everything slapdash. There is a large cross at one British base and naturally we asked its reason.

'Well, the man inspecting the dogs before turning in didn't clip a line to his belt. So, in the white-out, he lost his way. His companion stayed on all fours at the mouth of the tent, obviously shouting and shouting until he could shout no more. That's how he died, and that's how we found him, on all fours. The other fellow was never found. The dogs? Oh, yes, they were all right. Nothing wrong with them.'

If the tent fails the only life-preserving alternative for humans is an igloo. Admittedly the weather was dead calm, we had erected the tent, and there was no need whatsoever for my labours except curiosity, but I set to work with a shovel. The snow was wonderfully easy to dig, and blocks two feet long and one foot wide were manageable. These I fashioned into a circle and shaved the edges so that block met block more evenly. The next circle I shrank in size and, once again, did shovel shaves where necessary. It was hot work, and undoubtedly cooler in a blizzard when the wind whips up the snow (most blizzard snow comes from the ground rather than the heavens), but I was amazed how rapidly a dwelling could be formed. Mine ended more like a tall beehive, the sort of thing the Dinkas make for themselves around the Nile, and was certainly not the low dome it should have been—it is better, I learned, to build spirally rather than with concentric circles—but at least it was a home, locally made, impervious to wind, and there must be times when even friends would welcome and not mock such a crooked piece of work.

For driving the dogs it was necessary, if following the normal British method, to wear skis. If need be, and if the going is good, one can hold on to, or hook a belt on, or even ride upon the sledge. Instructions are given by word of mouth, a general euphemism for reaching to the bottom of your lungs and doing your damnedest to make the lead dog hear what it is you have in mind. Fortunately there are not too many options open. 'Go left' is a kind of r-r-r-r-r and most difficult to shout. 'Go right' is oink-oink and somewhat easier. 'Go forward' is almost anything, as they are probably doing that already, while 'Stop', the hardest of all, is a ridiculously gentle 'Ah no, ah no', sung in a quavering tone. It is said no more forcibly even when the ultimate confusion of a dogfight has broken out within the power unit. Jerking off your skis, saying 'Ah no' as if to a dancer who has just misjudged an *entrechat*, you hurry up to halt the fray. There are dogs and traces everywhere, much blood, a considerable mixing of bodies, great snarling and many teeth, but you are unbitten as you seize a collar and peg it with an ice-axe to the snow. This halts one dog and, if well chosen, may stop the fight. If not you find another ice-axe. And another, until there is a two-by-two order once again with considerable panting and licking of wounds.

When the system is working well, namely downhill and towards home, as with any horse, it is a delight. The nine wagging tails are all ahead and pulling well. The sledge's runners are sliding perfectly. Your foot is loosely on the brake, a plank that bends when you put some weight on it, and you r-r-r-r and you oink and they do go left and right.

Unfortunately, although they can withstand blizzards, and spend their lives staked out upon the snow, the economic climate will put them down. A 9-dog team can haul a ton of sledge for 30 miles a day on only 9 lb. of food. So far, so good, but a 9-dog team will also consume 9 lb. of food, sometimes seal-meat but also processed and expensive food, even when it does no work. A tractor uses fuel only when it is labouring and will continue to work unendingly, if need be. The calculations are in favour of tractors, not dogs. I am uncertain, having been unwilling to check, but I believe all the dogs I drove that day, and all their companions who yelped greetings as—in reasonable order—we arrived, have since been shot. There will not be the stench of seal-meat any more, but there will not be the pleasure of following, separating, feeding and being dependent on nine huge huskies for journeys away from home.

The American base on the peninsula had no dogs and never had had any. It had much of everything else—heat, food, drink, space, mechanical things, friendliness and garbage. Some computer must have hiccuped in sending supplies as a mountain of pigs' trotters and 9H pencils, still wrapped and packed, was dominant. The visitor resents a scene where objects thrown away are more conspicuous than everything in use, but this is a common feature of man—any man—in any wilderness. An African near Chad once told me he liked to see old cartons, old bottles lying by the way.

The things were reminders of people in so much space, and he preferred people to nothingness. Town litter is something else, for no one can forget people in a town, and no one wants their cast-off things; but in a wild place, where the wilderness is sufficiently triumphant, there is—or so it would seem—a compulsion to make a mark, any mark, upon it. The Eskimo leaves everything everywhere. The forest Indian will just abandon what he cannot take when he moves on. And, although I loathed those piles of cans (and saw even a discarded army tank on one such heap), I think the slovenly behaviour is actually accentuated by the wild miles of beauty on every other side.

The daunting size of Antarctica did take time to grasp. Walks were useful, as I lumbered and fell and then looked back to find, two hours later, that I had gone a mile. The boat trips helped, as more speedily we bumped and bored through the ice. Even journeys of ten miles or so, major endeavours out of sight of home, would help when their puny distances were etched upon a map. Most valuable of all, to me at least, were the journeys by air. The red twin-Otters would fly low and fast, and at first one could only note the wonder flashing by below, the sparkle from the sea, the crevasses and their depths, vast plains and mountainsides. At over a hundred miles an hour the world passed by, and then another thought began. Just how long would it take to traverse the area down below, each stretch so clearly full of covered cracks, each frightful heap of snow and ice?

We landed after one hour and our skis skidded to a stop not far from a tent, the first sign we had seen of anything to do with men. Its two occupants were a mapping party to whom we were making a delivery. Their dogs put huge paws upon our shoulders, licked us lavishly, and plainly they and the expedition were in good shape. But how long would it take them to travel straight back, without working on the way, to the place where they (and we) had started from?

'Oh, about six weeks; that's if we meet no snags.'

That evening, I extracted a good map of Antarctica and marked our journey on it. Most atlases relegate the entire continent to a page, and then fill it up with resounding names—Dronning Maud

Land, Novolazarevskaya, Prinsesse Ragnhild Kyst, Capitán Arturo Prat, King Leopold and Queen Astrid Coast, General Belgrano— to make it seem full and greatly occupied. It is not. In winter there are about 800 men collected into a score of settlements which, with or without their garbage heaps, are merely pinpricks. An average of one man per 7,000 square miles makes any ocean crowded by comparison. It means only seventeen men in the whole of the British Isles, all of them gathered in one spot, with two huts, one flag and a spike of aerials to keep them company. To go right across the continent, 2,800 miles at the widest point, would be to meet no other soul nor any sign that humans lived upon the Earth. It is also probable, save on the coastal fringes, that the traveller would see no other creature and no sign that creatures lived. It is hard for us elsewhere, so surrounded by living things, to think of the frozen emptiness within Antarctica. I looked at the line I had drawn on the map, a minute incursion into that barren land, a scratch and nothing more, and began to understand its size. Whether six swift weeks with the dogs, or one hour in a rapid plane, the line was pathetic. That night I threw my beer-can on the heap, and then another, for I knew that nothing of its kind lay over the hill. Just wildness. And beauty. And terrifying space.

The Antarctic has one final and unique quality that, for this book, is most relevant of all: no one owns it. Various countries did, to begin with, as they staked claims, announced sovereignty, and drew imperialistic lines across the emptiness. Then came the International Geophysical Year which, in eighteen months from the middle of 1957 to the end of 1958, proved that international co-operation could work and should continue to work. The spur had been the obvious blessings that science can achieve when like-minded men in different areas combine effectively. The IGY was a great success, especially in Antarctica. Consequently, great effort was made to prolong its internationalism. In 1959 the Antarctic Treaty was signed by all twelve nations actively involved on the continent. Essentially Argentina, Australia, Belgium, Chile, France, Japan, New Zealand, Norway, South Africa, Great Britain, the United States and the Soviet Union recognised it to be 'in the interest of all mankind that Antarctica shall continue forever to be used exclusively for peaceful purposes and shall not become the scene or object of international discord'.

Every other continent has been a battlefield of discord, with nationalisms dominating history. What a staggering exception to the rule it would prove to be if the last of the continents could manage to escape this ancient ritual. The actual clauses of the treaty are extremely straightforward and say, in effect, that all scientific information collected shall be freely exchanged; that nothing of a military nature shall be carried out; no nuclear weapons shall be exploded, however peacefully; no radioactive waste shall be dumped; all personnel shall move about freely; and that nothing anybody does shall give grounds for any claims to ownership. Following signature the treaty entered into force on 23 June 1961, with the intention that it should endure for thirty years thereafter.

Having run for half its time most successfully, and having had five more countries accede to its stipulations (Czechoslovakia, Denmark, Holland, Poland and Romania), questions arise concerning the second half and the years after 1991. The scientists have had the place very much to themselves so far. Will this be possible, or desirable, henceforth? Inevitably such a piece of land, however formidable, is not without natural resources. It has the largest coal reserves of anywhere in the world. (Scott picked up and carried some lumps on his sledge.) The peninsula, more investigated than other areas, is rich in minerals. There are great quantities of offshore oil and gas (estimated at 45 thousand million barrels of oil and 115 million million cubic feet of gas in the western part of the continental shelf alone). The treaty extends its influence up to 60°S and some kind of licensing for exploitation is being discussed more actively now than ever before. And more heatedly, because the energy lobbies are conflicting with the security lobbies, with both sets of arguments drowning the quieter remark that here is a piece of land where only science and nature have so far prevailed.

Each wilderness has its problems. The Antarctic, exceptional in so much, is no exception here. It is just, as they aptly say, that the treaty has 'frozen' all claims to ownership. Be that as it may, the

Wilderness

Antarctic is a wilderness and most of it will stay a wilderness, whatever immediate prospects are ahead. It will not suddenly cease to be the highest, windiest, coldest and most desolate continent, least endowed with life, just because some items of exploitation have come its way. They are digging up everything they can find in Canada and Australia, and yet those two countries are rich in wilderness.

On the night that we left the southern continent the sea crinkled as a new layer of ice formed on it. The frantic rush of summer, with life taking every advantage of the never-ending days, was coming to an end. The sun no longer missed but kissed the long horizon, and then sank beneath it as a portent of the darkness to come. We steamed north (where else?) and turned our backs upon those bergs and bergy bits to see what else this planet had in store.

3 *Forest*

Aqui não tem nada—here is nothing.
A Brazilian on seeing the forest
Here is everything.
The Indian who lives there

The axe bites deeply into the soft wood. It is then wrenched out
and made to bite again. More wrenchings, more cascades of
chippings, and a tree as tall as an English beech thunders to the
ground. Its death has taken one man with one axe precisely three
minutes. He moves on swiftly for he is on piece-work, paid by the
hectare of destruction he and his axe can cause. He disregards the
next tree, knowing its wood is almost as hard as the iron he carries,
then edges round a confusion of ants knocked from the security of
their leaf-ball home, and prepares to strike again. He pulls out a
Minister cigarette, lights it, extinguishes the match most carefully,
and then lifts his axe once more.

The place is the biggest tropical forest in the world. The precise
location is about a thousand miles south of the Amazon, half-way
between two of its biggest tributaries, the Araguaia and the
Xingú. The task on hand is the transformation of that forest scene
into the more profitable setting of a cattle ranch. For centuries the
area had been dormant, that is totally alive with creatures of the
great variety that live in South America, with equatorial plants of a

51

splendour and form that are often dazzling, and of course with people, with a black-haired, brown-skinned community of groups called, as with so many other kinds of men, the Indians.

Few are unmoved by their first encounter with the Amazon forest. 'The heavy resinous smells convinced me that I was in the presence of a superior order of vegetable things,' wrote a French traveller. 'Delight is a weak term', wrote Charles Darwin a century earlier, 'to express the feelings of a naturalist who, for the first time, has wandered by himself in a Brazilian forest . . . To a person fond of natural history, such a day brings with it a deeper pleasure than he can hope to experience again.'

'Stuff conservation,' said I when, advancing too casually into that assortment of vegetable things, I brought down a liana upon my back, dodged to avoid the immediate shower of ants and ended up against a tree barbed for protection more viciously than a mediaeval mace. Few forget their first encounter. If the visitor chooses to linger on the ground, admiring two-inch thorns that have just made mincemeat of a shirt, or looks reprimandingly at a liana now coiled as for Laocoön, he will not linger or remain unmoved for long. A roaming insect, astonished at such largesse, will sink a mandible or other implement at once, and so will all its tribe. The visitor has also arrived in the home of a superior order of predatory things.

It is easy to leave the axe-man at his work. If the sight is sad the best place to go is ahead of him into the old new world he is invading. There are still a million square miles of untouched forest in Brazil, ample to provide its atmosphere. A hundred yards will do. A mile will produce a whole trail of memories, and a journey of ten miles will induce a longing to retrace one's steps, wherever they may be. Actual walking is usually not difficult. It becomes worse where the light shines through to boost the undergrowth, but for the most part progress is no harder than in an English copse. However, unlike people in England, one carries a *facão*. This is of the same genus as a machete and a panga, a blade of steel for thwacking, chopping, cutting, slicing, gouging, probing, prising. Indeed, one wonders, after being in a locality that lives by them, how other areas can survive without these essential tools.

With a *facão* one is not omnipotent but a lot less impotent. It parts a way, and clears a path, and just occasionally, if your aim has not been true, will bring down a great liana on your un-suspecting back.

To many the Amazon forest was as near to hell as their minds could contemplate. To the Indians it was the great provider, the only provider, but for an invader it was often just a very nasty piece of country. It could weigh down upon him, giving no respite. It prevents those long-range views that can refresh the spirit. It is enormous, and seems infinite. And, of course, everything meets at the top, giving the individual far below a claustrophobia, a sense of submergence, an urgency—should fear grip him—to flee at once.

The *bandeirantes* were the first to invade, the robber-explorers who went for knowledge and easy pickings but, whether they found either, came back with strings of Indian ears about their belts. They never damaged the forest; there was no point in doing so. When the *seringueiros* followed, tapping the tall *Hevea* trees for latex wherever they found them, and desperately in debt to their sponsors, they too shot at the Indians, but they also did no harm to that eternity of trees. Like the prospectors they were content to stay alive, escape the Indians and eventually leave the forest, preferably for good. It had no more merit in their eyes than does the bran in a bran-tub. It was material through which and in which to locate a modest affluence.

Today's traveller does not require imagination to find out what it was like. He only needs a face for the thorns to thwack at, eyes and ears for flies to enter, a navel for the ticks, and a body to take hot note of all these punishments. The earlier voyager probably started off with a working knowledge of fleas, lice and other extras to his life, and merely exchanged one population for another as he reached into the interior. Today's visitor, less versed in such matters, finds the assault amazingly impressive. There are flies that head straight for eyes, attracted by the moisture. There are small bees and others that revel in nostrils, gaining swift access and liberating a tremendous smell when they die, as die they must— by a swift squeeze—to halt the tickling. Others walk into ears, surmount the hairy wax, and climb the smooth and nerveless portion that then follows before leaping up and down upon that trampoline that is the tympanum. To have two ears hammering in this fashion is to go rapidly berserk. I cannot think why torturers have not explored its possibilities.

There are also flies that bite and work, as it were, in shifts. In the daytime, notably in full sunlight, the *pium* hover permanently in the nearby air. They attack whenever bare skin and opportunity present themselves, and only later does the victim know how badly they have struck. In the evening there are mosquitoes (relatively few) and the invisible *maruim* (multitudinous, judging from the blotchiness they cause). A pox will suddenly have struck each unwary, bare-armed victim. At night both *maruim* and *pium* relent, having gorged sufficiently, but *Psychodid* sandflies take to the air as immediate replacements; they bite in the darkness and leave an itchiness beyond compare. At all times, but mainly in the warmth of day, ticks will complement the insect predators, dropping on or climbing up all passing humans with extreme ability, seeking out moist areas near the waist and crowding into every navel in particular until it overflows. 'Save Water: Shower with a Friend' ran slogans in New York one hot dry summer. Shower with a friend in central Brazil and pull off each other's ticks before they dig in too far. The creatures come, incidentally, in three sizes. The largest are the easiest to remove, there being no problem in catching hold of them. The smallest are the most vexing. Two hundred can pack themselves into one modest umbilicus. I can assure you of that fact, but no one bothers to count after the first such exercise.

The plants can also strike. Nine out of ten ferns are as soft in their fronds as ferns should be. The tenth can have two-inch black spines set along their leaves and up their stems. No spot seems to have been left unspined; the display is awesome to observe. There are also sedges, innocent in appearance, but sufficiently sharp-edged to slice a man's cornea should he happen to fall awkwardly. And what other way is there to fall when, with feet caught in some trailing tendril, and hands recoiling from a ferny porcupine, one tumbles to the ground?

Naturally there are counterbalancing delights. There is the joy of finding a river and the greater happiness of sailing down it. You see tapirs, more like horses when in the water but creatures from the Eocene when out of it. There are capybaras, famous as the largest of all rodents. And on the banks are *jacaré*, called neither crocodile nor alligator but cayman. Above, and away from the confusion of the trees, it is easier to see parrots and macaws or a glint from the huge beak of a toucan flying through the air.

I journeyed down the Suiá Missú, an 800-mile river of no great consequence, save that it is beautiful, bright clear with fish, bulging with sandbanks at every bend, garlanded with trees, and forever flown over by birds that shriek or swoop or cry their names at you. I spent days on this river, watching a half-Indian named Andrelinho catch fish with each throw of the line, pull them in, cut streaks in them, rub in salt, and then toast them over open fires. I bathed, watched turtles struggle to their perches along a branch, stalked caymans, and saw capybaras leap like antelopes in the water beneath the boat. The nights too were excellent. There was the fire, the taste of fish, much warm sand beneath and nothing to disturb the sense of peace.

That was the rub. It had been Indian country and was no more. They had gone. That whole river, as bountiful as any, had been stripped by one circumstance or another of all its humankind. They had died or vanished and, for the time being, Andrelinho and I were its sole inheritors. There was that length of river and, except for the beasts, we were its kings. I can think of no more wondrous a location than a *praia*, or sandbank, and no task more soothing than moving round when the fish smoke chooses to come your way; but there was too much sadness in all that emptiness. I have no more wish than the next person, be he rubber tapper or backwoodsman, to feel the sharp knock of a club upon my head, and then to have my body decked, however prettily, with arrows and other ornaments in honour of my going. I prefer Andrelinho's style of company but, as I munched his fish and then lay supine looking at the stars, I knew I had no right to such lonely emptiness.

There should, for example, have been the Xavante. They had been among the most feared of Indian tribes, allegedly leaving their footprints in reverse to confuse pursuers. One day, when I was hot, weary from a road journey, unwilling to leave the car's front seat, and gazing at a tabanid fly buzzing on the glass, a face appeared suddenly in the space beyond. It was broad, fairly dark, and above the eyes was a fringe. On top the hair was close cut but it hung down behind like the shade flap of a kepi. The man was wearing clothes, untidily and unfittingly as if these things were a misfit in themselves. Within the T-shirt, distorting it hopelessly, was a body of immense strength, and even the feet at the bottom end of unkempt trousers were more vast and solid than any I had seen. He was smoking and suggested I should give him tobacco. Failing that, what about matches, *fósforos*? Failing them, what about fish-hooks or line or ·22 bullets? *Vinci-dois*, boom boom, *macacu matou*, he elaborated, and then stroked the tyre with his foot. They looked of similar material.

It was in the 1940s that the Xavante had collapsed. By then parachutists were clearing airstrips in their area, small planes were landing, ground parties were linking these outposts with a chain of narrow *picadas* along which men could walk with ease. The noise of the *machada* and *facão* was everywhere, cutting at the forest, and Portuguese began to replace the halting, epiglottal sound that is Xavante talk. Gradually it became known that the fighting had finished without any final battle. Before long the former warriors were wandering peaceably into the new villages being built on their land and it was in Xavantina, aptly and wretchedly named, that I saw that fringe-haired barrel of a man whose tribal name had instilled such fear.

A day or so later I went with him to the *aldeia* of an encampment where he lived at the junction of two rivers. From afar it looked as a Xavante village should look, with a circle of beehive huts, small cooking-fires by each of them, plantations of bananas,

---

The largest tropical forest of modern times covers much of Brazil, just as moss covers a rock, and the rivers weave their way through it. The Suiá Missú of Mato Grosso and, overleaf, Spoonbill, Scarlet ibis, a Karajá Indian, and one of the new roads that will destroy the ancient way for ever.

manioc and urucu close by. From nearer, and not too near at that, its sameness began to wane. The tattered clothes were everywhere. The huts reeked with coughs and indolence, and the few dogs did not bark. My host was kind enough, but I did not stay and soon paddled once more along the Rio das Mortes, the river that had been a frontier for so long.

Nearby, just thirty minutes' ride in a Dakota, there are other Indians shielded by land legislation from what has been called the trauma of excessive contact. They know there is another world beyond their own. They see visitors and the condensation trails of aircraft. They watch the night sky, now flickering when the toppling remains of rocketry pass silently in orbit. On earth their rituals are rich. They wrestle. They hunt and fish. They paint their bodies, make necklaces fron rectangles of snail shell or claws of jaguars. Some distort their lips with wooden discs, or tie tight thongs to make their muscles bulge. They keep eagles for the feathers; they dance, and are kind and cruel to each other in their fashion, not ours. They can bury alive those who transgress. They keep to their ancient ways and we, they feel, can keep to ours.

A sick Waurá from this Xingú world was once taken by Kenneth Brecher, a friend I am proud to know, for treatment in São Paulo. It was from the jungle of trees to the dusty turmoil of a city in one brief hop by plane. Everything was new. The young man held Brecher's hand, straining to comprehend, sleeping in a bed, meeting toilets, observing the police with guns.

'They are the men of the chief,' said Brecher.

'The chief cannot be a real chief,' replied his companion, 'or he would not need men to guard him.'

On leaving São Paulo the young Waurá said he would not disclose what he had seen either to his tribe or to his own chief.

'He is an old man and it is better that he does not know. Perhaps one day I will tell my son. Perhaps not.'

Our own rules and way of living, unavoidable from the moment

Above, giant water lilies and, below, the pattern of pantanal where small hummocks of land, complete with termite mounds and trees, manage to stay above each flood.

of our birth, have dominated both us and the planet. 'Other societies may not be better than our own,' said Lévi-Strauss; 'even if we believe them to be so we have no way of proving it. But knowing them better does nonetheless help us to detach ourselves from our own society.' There were 3 million Indians in the land to be called Brazil, or so it is thought, when European man first set his booted foot upon it. There are now, or so it is feared, just 60,000 representatives of those earlier inhabitants. It is difficult to know them better when they have all but vanished from the scene. The forest is still full of life but its people have largely gone and the place has an emptiness that some feel must be filled. It is a vacuum, in its way, and therefore intolerable.

The axe bit deep into the bark of another tree. Its owner briefly left it there, paused while he put out his Minister cigarette, pushed the stub carefully into some moss, and then gripped the straight and sweaty handle once again. He was on piece-work, after all. On every side of him, quite apart from the devastation he had caused, were forty colleagues, each wielding nothing technologically more advanced than an axe. They would shout if a particularly big tree was about to fall. Otherwise it was up to each man to keep at a sensible distance and to fell each tree away from any neighbour.

Not only were the hard ones disregarded, and left upright in the chaos, but so were those with wasps in them. South America is the home of more wasp genera than all the rest of the world and some of their nests look as frightening as indeed they are. There are small kinds, made as if with concrete, and others four feet tall that hang high and, should their trees be knocked, will pour forth clusters of wasps, clinging together for speedier exit from the central ventral hole. Then, like a parachutist pulling his cord, they stop their downward plunge and hurry off to seek and punish the transgressor. They tend to search only the general area of their nest, but if that nest is felled to the ground they will meet up with the axe-men and these men, however speedily they run, will not be fast enough. Many of the species can be lethal. They are, or can be, a greater hazard than some falling giant of a tree. They are almost as fearful as an ill-placed cigarette.

The purpose of this destruction is, as the men over in the eastern cities put it, *derrubar*. It is clearance. Those with the axes, it would at first appear, achieve the very opposite in creating entanglement from the relative order of standing trees; but they also use a match. That is struck in August, the year's driest month, when all the fallen timber is like tinder and a single match will do. In the meantime, they continue to chop, to look warily up, to lay their trees with skill, to fell the hundreds of hectares that are their lot.

They do not own the land and never will. They do not and cannot even rent it. Such things are in the hands of city men. For centuries people have been buying and selling huge plots of space in central South America, but without any thought that they might actually handle these possessions. It was as if their plots were on the moon. Quite suddenly the situation changed. Brazil wished to make more use of its enormous hinterland. It moved its capital from Rio to Brasilia, a leap of 600 miles into the interior. It planned great roads, from north to south, from east to west, and found the money for them. Therefore, instead of some purchase being a number inscribed upon a map of heaven knows where, it began to represent an actual piece of land. The brave new road grew nearer and nearer until, one day, it was close enough for that number to be accessible. A way to the moon had been found.

'Stuff conservation,' I had said, when falling entangled to the ground. 'Stuff it all,' I had added, as the ants began to bite; 'stuff the lot of it.' And that, more or less, is what is happening to the greatest tropical forest of them all. The pieces of land involved in the transactions from the past have not been small. They are not the quarters of one square mile awarded to the North American homesteaders when they and their families set out to tame their continent. By and large the plots in southern America are several thousand times bigger. Half a million acres, a million acres—provided you had sufficient pence per acre (and the prices then were modest in the extreme) you could take your pick.

When the road had approached sufficiently near to your entitlement you hired a team of men. Their first task was to make some kind of track (road being too grandiose a term) between the government's highway (that too is an unpaved thing) and your piece of ground. The axe and the *facão*, together with a team of forty men to use them, are sufficient to create a few miles of track every day. On completing the distance, and having taken note of the place's disposition, you set the men to work. It is helpful to have a plane, and to fly over the estate, because it is 30 miles by 30 miles, or thereabouts. It must be fascinating to observe its layout for the first time, its streams, hills, regions of rock and other attributes. No one has ever mapped it from the ground and the only facts have come from aerial surveys—useful, but a partial truth. From your vantage point, and aided by the map, you then choose a starting-place, plus a possible site for the village-to-be, a spot for the sawmill, for your house, for a hotel, for anything you have in mind.

For everything the first necessity is to destroy what has been standing for so long. The men work diligently (two-fifths of their pay is taken for board and lodging) but the size of your inheritance is so vast that they only dent it during the first season. The trees are cut from the end of the rains (April) until the height of the drought (August). It is then the time for a match. Everyone has been warned. Only a madman would be within the felled area on that fearful day.

The result of the match is terrifying. There is no problem about the flame catching in that bone-dry time of year and, within an hour at most, the holocaust has travelled through all the cut square miles. It rages no further, as it cannot catch the living stands of trees, but it kills all those the axe-men found too hard. They stand, when the fire has passed, stripped of leaves, of bark, of life. Above them the smoke rises thousands of feet into the air. Pilots say that flying in central Brazil is 'very difficult' during this time of year. And so indeed it must be because this funeral pyre is not of logs taken from a forest but of the forest itself.

To walk into the devastation, once the heat has cooled sufficiently, is to cry. There is no other way. The termite mounds still glow, as if fresh from a kiln. The stumps of trees all smoke like little furnaces. Everywhere there are signs of the old jungle—a liana fragment, an ant trail, a huge fungus that has withstood the flame—but everywhere is death. One does cry; there is just nothing else to do.

By no means has everything burned to ashes. It takes more than one raging horror to destroy a forest. The standing trees still stand, however bereft of company. The fallen trunks have fallen further, as supporting branches were consumed, and they lie this way and that across the ground. Some of them will burn for weeks, if the fire has caught hold of a soft interior, but such small curls of smoke form the only movement to be seen. There are no leaves or twigs to catch the breeze. There are no birds because, although they at least will have flown away, there is nothing left for them to eat, no seeds, no fruits, not even any insects to tempt them back again. No men died, but a forest did. It met its Passchendaele.

In destroying the trees the fire liberated their stored-up minerals. Consequently, nature being what it is, there is a rush to make use of them, an invasion of weeds, a secondary growth of extreme energy. Moreover, as August is followed by a season of rain, intermittent at first but then more steady, the new plants have both water and all those elements to slake their needs. In time, a few months at most, it would seem as if the wound were healed, there being such a covering of green over both the land and all those angled columns that once were trees; but then the rain dries up. The new growth cannot flourish any more. It withers and turns brown. By the time August arrives once again everything is brittle-dry. It is therefore occasion for yet another match.

This time the fire seems fiercer still, for it almost runs over the ground; but there is less meat for it than previously and less power in consequence. Nevertheless, it destroys the secondary growth, reduces the great trunks lying on the ground, and eats at the boles of those still standing until many of them fall down. Growth will then start again, with the same short-sighted vigour as before, and the subsequent drought will come no less assuredly. A third match, another conflagration, a further reduction of all those stark reminders of the forest, and the place begins to look more like a field which, of course, has been the intention all along.

It is hardly a field to European eyes, as the largest of the trunks have refused to go away, but the grass that is sown is even less of the European kind. This is planted in clumps, a few feet apart, and these soon stand well above head height. It is then time to introduce the object of all the labour so far expended on its behalf—the cow. Dwarfed by the grass, diverted by the great trees still lying there, and tripped by the old cores of termite mounds, the cow plods over this brand-new land, this colossal kingdom come its way.

I asked to make a tour of the cow's domain and they put me on a horse, the better to see the place. Gone was the need for a *facão*. Now it was a matter of open land and four hooves. Normally, let it be admitted at the outset, I and a horse are like bread and water, each more tolerable on its own than mixed. Whenever and however I approach a horse there is someone who will say, 'Not done much riding then?' This is long before I have even hesitated about which foot to put into the stirrup. Anyway, I have found that horses only come in two categories. Either, on the opening of the stable door, they break loose in a straight gallop or, however much I urge and coax them, they move as if their years and my weight are jointly unacceptable.

The mount they offered at the *fazenda* was at least small; I prefer them that way. There were many ticks about its tail, all of the large variety, and I felt a twinge of sympathy. I was right first time with my left foot and no one had opportunity to say 'Não tem montado muito?' before the gate was opened and off we went. A small boy was on a smaller horse grazing peaceably as I hurtled by, but my charge was infectious and soon the lad and his beast were galloping next to mine. Unfortunately, he was also screaming. He was hating every moment and making the point with unbelievable vigour.

John Hillaby, so he writes, has a projectionist within his skull who clicks on short one-reelers from time to time. I was suddenly witness to such a screening. It was all perfectly clear. There was I and there was the lad. There was my strong right arm and his plaintive situation. By leaning over at an astonishing angle, and by stretching my arm to seven feet or so, I was able to grasp his shaking shoulders, utter a soothing word and flick him from his steed to mine. There was a mother, bright-eyed, brown-limbed, warm with gratitude, and then the reel clattered to its close, leaving me and the lad still thundering along. My projectionist was just about to put on another short (which would have shown me scooping up the fallen rein) when the boy, very sensibly and very gracefully, fell off to land in a clump of Mato Grosso grass. He suffered but a single scratch. I was even more unscathed.

The point of this shaming interlude is that we had time to cover an enormous distance. Moreover, we had covered it in a straight line and we could have continued, had the boy's wisdom not prevailed, for much longer. Such facts may be unremarkable in other parts of the world, but the land over which we galloped so directly had been forest not four years before. The horizon was still forest on every side, sharp-edged like a half cut field of corn, but the ten miles by ten miles lying in between was now a ranch. It was along its major road that the boy and I had travelled with such unnerving haste.

The gallop improved my horse. Thereafter she was a most responsive creature. Together we went over that ranch for as long as the day allowed. All its roads were lined with wire fences, and most of the stakes were black on one side as reminders of the fire. there were a few stag-headed trees still standing—dead, smooth without their bark, stark and no longer of consequence. They made no shade for the tall grass growing down below, the *capim coloniāo*, whose tussocks make such dramatic use of the forest's minerals. We travelled through it, my horse and I, and the grass rasped against us. If I stood in the stirrups I could see above its coarse brown growth. If not, she and I were completely lost from view.

Then we met the cattle. There was a herd of about one thousand head. They were all white, well horned, and flabby as zebus and brahmins are with a camel-hump of fat above their necks. They were not wide-bodied, like European beasts; but, for tropical creatures, they were in very good shape. Many of them had been crossed with the great Chianina stock from Italy. The intention had been to create the double blessing of beasts able to survive such conditions and also able to produce a lot of meat. Sometimes in the tropics, as I was later to wonder in northern Kenya, there

63

seems no point in killing a cow, so little meat must exist between the skin and the bone. Not so on this *fazenda*. The forest was becoming steaks with extreme rapidity.

The scale of the operation was impressive. My horse and I were roaming on a million-acre ranch. So far only 64,000 acres had been cut down and 20,000 head were grazing on them. The axes would clear another 20,000 acres each year, that being the extent of each August fire. The cattle were purchased wherever possible, and then walked westwards from their ranches in the east. One sometimes met a herd of several thousand, lowing, eating, slowly travelling, as they followed the man with a huge horn somewhere at the front. In would take time passing such an obstacle, but one began to learn something of the size of this form of business. Each large ranch wishes to create about 100,000 head before it is ready to commence slaughtering. Finding such quantities of beasts, particularly when everyone else has the same idea in mind, is difficult. Therefore every ranch is equally enthusiastic about breeding from the animals already in its possession, and great canisters of frozen sperm are flown in repeatedly. Even so, one cow can only be made to produce one calf in a year, and half of those calves will be relatively unwelcome males.

My horse proved beautifully adept at finding a way through the various enormous herds lying in our path while I absorbed the scale of this solitary ranch. In time, which will not be long whatever the obstacles, the population of 100,000 head will be achieved and about 200,000 acres of the Amazon forest will have been felled, burned and re-burned for its benefit. Then the slaughter will begin. The black vultures now seen hovering in the sky, always ready to feed should a cow die down below, will line up in regiments when that day comes. The plan on each large ranch is to kill 200 animals every day of the year. Their carcases will be flown out by air and each settlement has already found a site, if not a work-force and levelling gear, for its 3,000-metre runway. There is even a plan, as attractive in its simplicity as the axe, for walking the beasts into the freighters, killing them there, and leaving the cabin unpressurised when the plane takes off once more. A height of 30,000 feet is quite cold enough to refrigerate the entire consignment before it arrives, stiff and ready for storage, at some rich city in the east. Or in North America. Or in Europe. The *fazendeiros* who run these ranches are not thinking small thoughts. 'We', said one, 'will feed the world.'

I had suddenly seen enough. This time we galloped at my request. Beneath her hooves the soft dust, as fine as baby powder, was flicked into the air. If there was a wind it would blow away, just as the prairies to the north had blown away so that New Yorkers complained of the dust; but Brazil is lucky in having little wind. However there is rain, and undoubtedly much of this earth will find its way into the rivers; but Brazil is lucky in having land so flat. The deep gullies of erosion will appear but not as they do in steeper countrysides. No one quite knows what will happen and whether such good fortune will be enough. The soil was never rich; only the death of the forest has briefly made it so. The minerals had been collected for millennia, stored in the wood, and now all that capital has been exposed. The grass is quick to profit. So too the cows. So, doubtless, all those rich men in the east.

We reached the place where the old trees still stood tall. I looked back at the ranch. Our dusty trail was very plain, still hanging in the air, with not a breath to blow it away. We found a *picada* and were soon engulfed in the shade and silence of the ranch's former ownership. After a while I had to walk, the pathway having a low branching roof, and the horse clopped along behind, without the need to hold her reins. A monkey chattered high up, the capuchin kind with a tonsure of white upon its head. And then silence again, save for hooves upon leaves often as brittle as papadoms. We skirted an ant's nest, overflowing on the path. It was of *Atta sextus*, whose distinction lies in making quite the biggest dwelling of any ant. This one was fully twenty feet across. Its highways teemed with occupants, boringly busy. Not one ant stopped for more than a second at any time, and only then if there was cause, a need for recognition, an obstacle, a dead one in the way. I and the horse walked round and on.

A gorgeous woodpecker, red, bright red, swooped down through the trees. Another bird, extraordinarily decked, also flew and became a pigeon the moment it did so. Very often a bird will

65

not reveal its kind, so to speak, until it flies. The woodpecker was unmistakable the moment it took off; so too that over-decorated dove. Flying between the continents, as I was to do so much, could reveal the variation between species most explicitly. A woodpecker, wrong in colour to European eyes, wrong in size, wrong in the sound it made, could in fact be nothing else. It is even more wrong to mention Darwin or Wallace in the same breath as oneself, but I could begin to see how their own leap-frogging about the world had been vital to their thinking. It is static to know, as many naturalists do, all about one locality. To move is to see both variation and isolation, the crucial ingredients of evolution. I think, with all the wisdom of one who already has the answer, that the theory of natural selection could only have been first proposed by such movers about the planet as those two men.

We reached a river. The horse drank and I took off my clothes. There are two facts that everyone knows about South America. One is that it has tarantulas, swifter and no less lethal than the worst of all the snakes. The other is that rivers are rich with piranha, ready to pick a man to his bones in minutes or, if blood has maddened them beforehand, in little more than seconds. I too had been aware of both these certainties.

Inquiry about the first of these facts led me to visit a certain city arachnologist whose room was filled with living spiders. Each book-like box was on a shelf, labelled and correctly occupied. He showed me first the biggest, a group of creatures so large that they could fit only half their legs upon my open palm. They would stumble, having misplaced the other half, but would never bite, or so my host assured me repeatedly because such assurances can do with second tellings. A general rule for venomous spiders, he said, is that the larger they are the less powerful the punch they pack. With that he produced a box with care, a mannerism I had not noticed earlier. In it was a spider, the size of a double pin-head, and the moment it moved the lid was quickly closed. That individual, he told me (and, by contrast, there are times when one telling is adequate), was the most lethal in his entire collection. 'Watch out for it,' he added; 'there should be plenty where you're going.'

I did find tarantulas and occasionally dug them up when they had scurried into holes. As for their smaller brethren, I had no idea how either to find them or avoid them; it seemed they held all the cards, including the most effective trump of all. On the other hand, I could find piranhas, and did so frequently. Moreover I, no master with a rod and line, or even a *brasileira* with a line without a rod, could catch them frequently. It was the type of fishing only fishermen despise. First find some meat. Hook it to the line. Cast, or at least make the meat fall somewhere other than on land. Pause for a count of two. Then, hand over hand, pull in the line and the fish.

Far harder than catching the piranha was removing them from the hook without being rasped in the struggle by their teeth. These are indeed worthy of their reputation. They are as serrated, orderly and sharp as mere teeth could ever be. They are not paticu-larly big, but then neither are razors, needles, rapiers, or, for that matter, fangs. There is more than once species of piranha, but the kind I caught, wrestled with on land, and ate with pleasure (though most prefer a rarer kind of fish known as tucunaré) were about 8 inches long, 6 inches high and 1 inch fat. Their teeth were the size of those on a carpenter's saw. However, I could believe that given time and steadfastness of aim they could sever anything they chose.

For example, me. Having placed my clothes on a rock away from ants and termites, I prepared to immerse myself. Admittedly, I had not fished these waters, but the river was as wide and clear as others where, on different days, I had speedily proved the existence of piranha. I did not doubt their presence in the shallow clarity ahead of me. Nevertheless, I had been assured that the event of piranha consuming a man is so rare as to be discountable. Of course, the local people added, it is foolish to tempt the fish with blood because this steps up the odds, but the circumstance of a fish eating a man is still fairly rare. I looked at my legs. They drooled, one way and another, with blood. They always do in an insect-rich environment, where a score of scabs can be scraped with each excoriating scratch. The blood had congealed but it was reasonable to expect that any predatory creature geared to live, if not by blood alone, at least by meat would detect even a modest trace of it.

I looked at my horse, hoping for some innate guidance. She gave none, and concentrated on biting at her own scabs. A sun-bittern landed on the bank nearby, with a disarming scurry of noise. A flights of ducks went upstream, Muscovy ducks, and I speculated on that name in such a continent. I also wondered if the horse would return riderless to her stable should I fail to surface from the swim. Hillaby's projectionist was at work again. So I dived, and there was indeed a sudden stab of pain.

Never having been nibbled to extinction I was uncertain about the immediate sensation, but the undeniable pain that arose was, I only slowly realised, from a bad dive. So, happy and quite unnibbled, I swam about. Two hyacinth macaws, rarest and most beautiful, sailed overhead. Another flights of ducks came by (Muscovy in this context is, I discovered later, a corruption for musk, the original name being Musk duck.) A turtle plopped straight off its branch. A sting-ray, harmless for those who stick to swimming, idled past and lost itself in the ripples and riffles—for so the shallow parts are called—that stretched ahead of me. The horse, I noticed now, had waded into the water. Just who had been watching for innate guidance? (Which abruptly reminds me of the tale about Eskimos building thicker igloos in a recent year. An American, based nearby, suspecting some sixth sense, asked the cause. 'We see you bringing in double the fuel this time,' an Eskimo replied.)

I returned to the horse and sat in the water washing her scabs. The sun was low down, hesitating before making its final plunge. A great group of kingfishers flew into the trees above and then leaped off again, skimming the water before swooping up on the river's other side. Could anything be more perfect? Yes is the immediate answer, for at that moment I suddenly remembered the *candiru*. Remember the *candiru*, they had said, and I had clearly failed. Time would tell how grave the lapse had been. These small and well-barbed fish, so I was told, would climb into any orifice. They normally live in the sand at the shore. My various sphincters tightened at the thought and I dressed with idiotic haste. Later, firm in the saddle and cantering for home, I could smile at the likelihood. I wondered if it were called a bottom-feeder as so many fishes are. I even laughed out loud, I regret to say, before galloping back along that selfsame road where I and the lad had thundered just half a dozen hours before.

That night and the next day there was a tremendous storm. Just how do the tropics produce such sheets of water? I had read of a place that suffers an inch of rain an hour for many days, and I looked through the waterspouts coming off the roof with astonishment. Somewhere in that storm, so we had been informed by the crackling radio, there was the boss of the huge *fazenda* that I had been inspecting. He too was paying a visit, not that there was much of it to be seen at the moment, beyond the red-mud street, the row of whitewashed homes, and the wind-sock hanging heavily at the end of a runway as red and muddy as almost every-thing else. The view was minimal; but, for the occupants of any plane above, it must have been even less far-ranging. I could not imagine how they hoped to arrive, let alone to land.

Suddenly there was a purring roar just above the house. We looked and saw nothing. The sound vanished and, curious as we were to see the boss, we hoped he would fly on and land some-where else. The end of the runway was already marked by the carcase of a plane whose owner, as the last thing he did, had suffered from misjudgement. How the boss's pilot did it I do not know, but the next thing that we saw, squelching through the mud and flicking red water in its wake, was a twin-engined plane securely on the ground. Misty figures were waving from within while we waved back from our security. We knew this *fazendeiro* lived in São Paulo, held bank directorships, flew to Europe frequently, held further positions there, was married with many children, in his late thirties—and that was all, save that he and others like him were cutting down the forest of the Amazon. There was ample scope for prejudgement as he and the other occupants clambered from the plane to stand hunched beneath huge umbrellas. Worse still, I suddenly saw a revolver in the belt of the man who, from the deference he received, was plainly the one in charge.

Wilderness

It is, in its way, nice being wrong. I had singled out the right man and was also right about the gun, but he was not as prejudice had pictured him. For a financier he was ludicrously ebullient. Instead of a tight-lipped look there was a round and florid face, like an effusive and somewhat battered publican. He had two boils on his forehead, a hopeless shirt, a gaping pair of shoes, a look of poverty and a smile that reached deep into his eyes. I am not certain what language he spoke predominantly—Portuguese, Italian and English came out in disorder—but I know that none of us had difficulty in understanding every particle of what he said or, if words of all kinds failed him, what he meant to say. He was over-fat, rather small, and over-loud, and it was he who was chopping down that wilderness.

'We could not leave it,' he said. 'We could not neglect half of our country. We had to bring it into production. It was, how you say, come si chiama, oh damn it, I forget, but andiamo, vamos, let's go and look.'

So we went and saw. A truck appeared and we all climbed on it. There must have been a driver, for it lumbered forward, and there must have been another, for gates were opened as we passed, but there was a total torrent of talk to distract us from such things.

'I love the forest. Don't get me wrong. But it can't just stand there. We must make beef. We have people without food. Are you without food, senza mangiare? No, but you are not so fat as me.'

He was about to prod me, I feared, but the lorry lurched as an armadillo raced across the road. We needed one for the film. I leaped overboard, rushed through the *capim*, saw nothing, saw it beyond the fence, wriggled under the wire while still smarting at being called far, ran into the field, and then grabbed the animal's fast-retreating tail. There were little lines of hair by each band of carapace and the face was like a hedgehog's. I returned in modest triumph to find the engine and the talk still running.

'Nice tatu. I like tatu. They too are good to eat. They too will live because, you see, not all the forest will go. The government says we keep 50 per cent. So we keep 50 per cent. We will keep big pieces and small pieces. You see we like this idea. It holds the soil. It stops the wind. It keeps the water. And it means that we can go

70

hunting, jacaré, paca, onca perhaps, anta, mutum, macacu,' he said, and I remembered again the Xavante who had also expressed himself along such lines.

'What about the Indians?' I asked, pushing the armadillo into place with a foot. 'Could you bring them back at all, let them hunt, let them live again on the land?'

'No. What could they do? You see I was born in Naples. I know how to work. They don't. I leave Italy when I am seven. Now I am Brazilian and every day I work. They are not yet Brazilians, you know *brasileiro*, and they do not work.'

All the time we watched his ranch passing by. The stockmen, vastly skilful with their mules and horses, with ancient leather hats and always with spurs but often without shoes, had respect for the man from the east but never subservience. We saw inoculation and insemination, and disinfection of all the wounds. We watched the branding, red iron and white smoke. We saw, in short, what 10 million cruzeiros (£1 million) can do with a forest in five years, given determination, the energy of about a hundred men and the security of another 10 million cruzeiros waiting in the east to be spent in the next five years. Thereafter some money should start to flow the other way. At all times, whenever we looked, there was the horizon of trees. In part it looked like an army, massed for the attack. In truth one knew it could only retreat and there was no confidence that only half would do so. What about the years ahead, the bad years, or a political sop to the financiers? We looked back at the trees above the dust that flailed in our wake. The dust rose higher and higher, as a thunder-cloud will do, and soon the trees had vanished utterly. The boss also looked and then he too grew quiet. It was the only time that day that he did not talk.

On the following day I flew in the same two-engined plane on some errand to fetch a man. I had intended to take note of distance, direction, time and so forth, but forgot the very moment the wheels had left the ground. What a sight it was! Down on the ranch, and along the roads, it had been impossible to see over and above the trees. A kind of myopia had been dominant, a looking at all near things as if they alone existed. Up in the air the roads shrank into the faintest of scratches over the ground. Even the colossal ranch became the merest patch, a raft upon an ocean, a speck and nothing more. With the speed of the plane those ten miles by 10 miles were soon swallowed up and instead there was nothing but forest below.

If there were *picadas* or tracks down there we could not see them. Our view was solely of the tops of trees. Some bulged like chrysanthemums, thick with the yellow of their flowers. Others were no less bright, being blues and pinks predominantly, but these trees were less demanding or less successful at taking up space. Most were not in flower but even they were not a universal green. Some had recently shed their leaves, leaving bare brown limbs, and some had simply fallen, giving us dark glimpses of the world beneath. As for ticks or termites, ants or spiky ferns, it was hard to remember that they too were down there. Look at the sea when it is rich with waves, green and flecked with foam. It is easy to forget that every wave is full of plankton and all that surface water is rich with invisible life. So too those tops of trees.

The rivers were always a delight. When we flew low there was no hint of their coming. There was no apparent valley, no change in the style or kind of trees, but suddenly a flash of water would pass us by. We flew along one, looking for the porpoises that live at the union where one river meets another. We looked for cormorants whose black wings and long necks show up just as vividly as they do above the sea. We saw *praia* after *praia*, those glistening banks of sand heaped by the water as it meanders on its way. There were turtle tracks on them, and the marks where tapirs had clambered on to land. A plane flies at a nonsensical pace but there is an exhilaration at catching just a glimpse of things, a skimming fish, an otter and its wake, a scattered bunch of egrets, a heron proving yet again that flight can be achieved with dignity at a slowly measured pace.

In time we had to travel higher to look for the airstrip where we would find the man. It seemed a daunting task. On every side, and far beyond the circular horizon, there were trees. This was the Amazon forest—still. It was incredibly vast. With at least a million square miles of it standing in Brazil, with huge parts also reaching into Venezuela, Guyana, Colombia, Bolivia and Peru it was a

72

wilderness of gigantic proportions. More like an ocean than any kind of covered land, it was flat, turbulent in its fashion, entirely dominant and even frightening. We could sink beneath its waves, very easily. We could vanish just like a boat drowning in the sea. It was an alien thing down there, and not a part of us. Somehow, and I do not know why, it appeared as quite the biggest thing that I had ever seen.

Not so the airstrip. That was inexpressibly minute, just a hyphen on its own among the trees. We banked over to take a closer look, saw a group of men, and wondered if there was wind for us to land against. Once more we banked, straightened up, put down the flaps, lowered the wheels, and then side-slipped steeply to meet that streak of brown. We touched, bounced, touched again, and watched the tall wall of forest trees standing at the other end. Reverse pitch blew dust ahead of us and we stopped in time. One of the men approached, his head surrounded by a little swarm of *pium*.

'Tem *pium*?' we asked, and laughed before we too became embroiled.

'Tem,' he said. 'There are.'

That was about all there was, save for the group of men, one tarpaulin suspended on a frame, a few hammocks hung about, some rifles, and a softly smoking fire. All about were trees and it might have seemed as if the forest would soon repair this puny affront to its total embrace of the land, just as it speedily fills the space when a tall tree tumbles down. It was such a little runway and already there was green growth embedded in its brown.

It might have seemed that way, but we knew better. The man we had come to fetch climbed aboard and the others stood in a tiny group. They looked very small beside those giant trees, and almost pathetic. With one hand they were smoking cigarettes, puffing out purposefully against the wretched *pium*, and it might have appeared that we were condemning them to some fearful punishment, eventually to be engulfed in all that green. However, we did know better. In their other hand every single one of them held an axe. We also knew that most of them, if not all, would be absolutely bound to have a match.

4 *Desert*

Central Australia is so hot that its inhabitants have to live elsewhere.
Anon (at school)

Of course there were interludes between the parts of wilderness. It was impossible to move from one to another without encountering their very antithesis; but to re-enter the man-made configuration of a city was always confusing. Surely I left my passport inside this boot? And why cannot countries at least put their name on their currencies? How many of what are in an escudo or a peso, and what is this compressed milk-bottle top imprinted with a head upon, so to speak, its face? Surely Montevideo cannot be south of Buenos Aires, as the plane trip seemed to indicate, and why is this bus apparently heading for the desert instead of some city square?

To be blasé about travel means only that you have encountered enough earlier mishaps to lessen the sense of current embarrassment. I remember being very blasé in Brazil, talking of ticks and parasites in a most garrulous manner. The girl at the dinner table was partly to blame; her eyes widened and her nose twitched at each extravaganza of a tale. There had not been too many such eyes, noses, or even bodies, like that in the place where I had been. Later, I embraced even the men, before climbing into the taxi heading for the inevitable airport with the encircling scent of the evening still hanging over me. The sky looked blue, bright blue.

It then became black, jet black, and much, much wetter. I have never seen such rain.

The departure board clattered through all possibilities until 'Fechado' became the only word for each and every flight. The airport was closed and that, with the rain, was that.

What does the seasoned, worldly-wise globetrotter do in such circumstances? He makes for the bar. It is a good-humoured place, thick with people, thin with bartenders. Our accomplished traveller is finally served but then remembers how the taxi took the last of his local cash. He turns on his heel and meanders to the lavatory. It is full. Slowly he saunters out again. He takes deep interest in an advertising fork-lift truck. He is gently amused by a couple of hundred replicas of the concrete Christ of Corcavado. He toys with the idea of sitting down, but the seats are full and, judging from the refuse surrounding them, have been occupied for ever. So, bored out of his mind, he leans against a pillar to read 'Fechado' again and again. Only fresh clattering of the letters will give him a hint of future activity.

Then came the whine of a jet. The rain was easing and the girl at the desk returned, providing occasion to trot out a polished phrase: 'At what time, miss, will the aeroplane for Rio be departing?' She pointed, with gold finger-nails and a red pen, to the plane moving on the apron. I pointed a finger at the indicator board. She shrugged her shoulders and, with that mannerism which turns a pretty face into a prune, pursed her lips and turned away to deal with something near her foot.

Sentences became less coherent. When is next flight Rio? If that full when next? But other airline takes me other airport? How baggage get from one to other? Why not possible book here another flight Rio? Johannesburg? What where when connections over Atlantic? *Porque não tem esta* . . . and I petered out with everything suddenly very wrong. Everything—and this time there was no sauntering grace towards the lavatory as I hurried past the fork-lift truck, the concrete Christlets, the swing-door to sanctuary. Fortunately, not another soul was now within that place. Unfortunately, with time to ponder and a seat to ponder on, I realised I was sans effective ticket, baggage, any form of connection and all previous confidence. I looked for paper, used two hotel bills and a customs form, felt drained of life, and only with reluctance left that isolated cubicle. It was not until very much later, when halfway across the Atlantic and safely somewhere east of Rio, that I was able to laugh at the blasé traveller who first missed his plane and then chose that moment to have desperate need of an empty cubicle. The Greek word diarrhoea means 'I flow away'. What name more apt could there be?

However, to return to the matter of wilderness, the city dinner parties did also help to sort out thoughts. Given cause it was so easy to rattle on about insects, cold winds, hot winds, bad food, worse water and all the unwelcomeness of wilderness. To sit there, fondling some chilled white wine, comfortably attired and well filled, was to become steadily aware of a great gulf between this pleasure and that other world. I would talk at length, but knew in advance the reactions I would arouse.

'Masochist! You must be some sort of bloody masochist,' said the man, leaning across his stomach to take another morsel.

'Oh, no,' said his wife, 'it sounds wonderful,' and the grape she plucked was tendered to mauve lips.

A wilderness can indeed be wonderful but not, I felt, on her terms. It would first be necessary to extract its stings, cool or heat its air, and bring so much personal environment to it that its actual properties would no longer be recognisable. Is it masochistic to wish to see things differently, to know danger, to experience the natural world and not an emasculation of its reality? On the other hand is it idiotic to pretend anyone now is experiencing wilderness? For a start, one should be naked of everything the tamed world has to offer; but no one, however abstemious, travels without a considerable assortment of manufactured blessings, such as boots and food and instruments. To lack these is either uncomfortable, foolish or short-lived. Moreover, mankind being what it is, anyone arriving precipitately without equipment of any kind will quickly strive to put things right. The castaway will make a home in no time; that is the fault and wonder of man. So what of wilderness? If a visitor is present can it be one? A book of verse beneath a bough, a jug of wine, a loaf of bread, and thou singing in the where? Assuredly, with such a dearth of lack, it cannot be a wilderness.

On 300 occasions the word wilderness is used in the Bible and all the uses are derogatory, making it at best a spiritual gymnasium and at worst an absence of every desirable thing. To what extent have we shifted from that attitude, despite current blathering about the glory of nature? I wondered, and in wondering read widely to discover just when (or why) the change had occurred. A rock once upon a time had been good for shelter, for smashing into useful fragments—and for nothing more. Suddenly, for the poets at least, it became admirable merely for what it was, a hunk of nature, a thing untouched by man.

In the eighteenth century an English clergyman was despatched to the remote village of Elsdon in Northumberland. To his friends in the south he wrote that the landscape was covered by the purple flower of a plant called ling which made it 'indescribably hideous'. Later, when among the mountains of Scotland, he added that 'the summits of the highest are mostly destitute of earth; and the huge naked rocks, being just above the heath, produce the disagreeable appearance of a scabbed head ... If an inhabitant of the South of England were to be brought blindfolded into some narrow rocky hollow, enclosed with these horrid prospects, and there to have his bandage taken off, he would be ready to die with fear, as thinking it impossible he should ever get out to return to his native country.'

He had distinguished precedents for this view. Homer, living in a hilly, rocky region, commented enthusiastically on any flat areas. Lucretius said that mountains were to be avoided. Livy refers to 'foetidus Alpinum' while Cicero, a shade more generous, said any place of residence eventually becomes pleasing, 'even though it be a mountain or a forest'. Andrew Marvell called some mountains 'ill-designed excrescences that deform the earth and frighten heaven'. Thomas Gray thought Alpine scenery 'carries the permission of mountains to be frightful almost too far'. 'They fill the mind with an agreeable kind of horror,' added Addison. They are 'a magnificent horror', concluded Mme de Stael before closing her carriage curtains.

Are they not right in their way? There is great joy in striding forth upon a mountain, even—so far as one is able—upon its steeper slopes; but only so long as the home comforts last. When night falls, or cold strikes, or the food fails, those twinkling lights in the valley are as heaven. (Which is a reminder that Thomas Burnet bemoaned how the stars 'lie carelessly scattered as if they had been sown like seed' and thought 'what a beautiful hemisphere they would have made if they had been placed in rank and order'.) Even if a mountain walk has been one kind of heaven there is another in striding, tired and hungry, towards warmth and light and savoury smell. On the whole, most of us would sympathise with John Adams, America's second president: 'The whole continent was one continued dismal wilderness, the haunt of wolves and bears and more savage men. Now the forests are removed, the land covered with fields of corn, orchards bending with fruit, and the magnificent habitations of rational and civilised people.'

Eventually there came the new breed of men crying not in but for the wilderness. There were the English poets, walking, watching birds, writing odes to butterflies. They were no more in a wilderness than a man can be among the hedgerows and copses, hills and dales of England, but they started lines of thought that were entirely new. 'Some wilderness-plot, green and fountainous and unviolated by man,' wrote Coleridge. 'One impulse from a vernal wood', said Wordsworth, 'may teach you more of man, of moral evil and of good, than all the sages can.' Shelley wrote of 'Everything almost which is nature's, and may be untainted by man's misery'. Much of the credit for these new feelings should go to Jean-Jacques Rousseau, and to Diderot. They, and the nature poets who came after them, initiated the movement towards natural things. Even in the new United States, still abundant with wilderness, there was a rush to revel in the old days. Cooper, Audubon, Muir and Thoreau, in their stories, prints and sayings, proclaimed the past long before it all had gone.

Two questions put to me during my urban days struck with
particular power. I had been carrying on about the destruction of
the rain forest, and the poor exchange of a tree for a cow. I had
also been lauding the wonder of Antarctica, a continent so un-
trammelled, so wild and—as yet—unbruised. I argued that both
places were right merely because both places were as they had
always been. Then came the interjections.

'If not grass what else should be planted in Amazonia?'

'Where should the first hotel in Antarctica be situated?'

There was malice in those interruptions, but correctly so. I had
been to the places, and had seen them, but had not sufficiently
questioned my basic prejudices. It was far-fetched, I realised to
imagine that Antarctica could remain for ever as nothing more
than a frozen laboratory. It was equally vague to contemplate
Brazil leaving half the country to the wildness that had encased it
for so long.

The wilderness interludes both clarified and confused. It was
great to eat above the level of rice and beans but, faced with the
assertion that wilderness living is without merit, I suddenly longed
for rice and beans once more. Conversely, when confronted with
the stricture that only nature is beautiful, it was easy to disagree,
to resent the dictum that everything in a city is second-rate if set
against a field, a wood or a single tree. To ask nowadays for the
world's wonders is to be answered, not with seven man-made
things as in ancient times but with natural marvels. The Sistine
Chapel is less than a blade of grass, a Michelangelo lower than one
skylark pounding its wings against the sky. Dull must be he of
soul, or so I mused in city luxuries, who sees all artefacts as things
inferior to the great slurry of nature from which they sprang.

By the time I reached central Australia I was considerably more
disordered than at the outset of the world wilderness tour. I knew
well enough that I still wished to see wild emptiness—hence the
mad rush that quickly found me recumbent beneath a muddy
machine—but I did not possess such conviction as formerly.
Besides, the new area was a desert. 'Put your money into
land, son, because they're making no more of it,' says ancient

advice; but deserts are different. There are still plenty of them.

Add together the big deserts, the Sahara, Arabia, Turkestan, Thar, Gobi and Colorado, all in the northern hemisphere, and the total is 4½ million square miles. Add also the southern deserts, Kalahari, Australia, Chile, Argentina, and the sum adds up to over 6 million square miles. Add the smaller places, no less dry but less well known, and the total is 7 million, or 12 per cent of the total land surface. And finally the great areas of semi-desert, not dry enough to be true desert but hopeless for agriculture, and the proportion rises to 16 per cent of the whole. It would seem as if no tears need be shed for the desert wilderness. 'Don't put your money in deserts, son; they're still making them.'

I went to Australia because it possessed the largest desert in the southern hemisphere and I was ignorant of it. Just what did it provide? Almost at once it offered Ernest Giles. If also offered million-acre farms with only 3,000 head of cattle on them, extraordinary rocks like Ayers and the Olgas, the most poisonous collection of snakes in the world, and rivers with everything rivers should have—banks, meanders, sandy bottoms—save for water. These dry shapes wandered from one horizon to the other, as if searching for the element to make them whole again, and they seemed to come from another age, when water was rife, when rivers ran with fish. The land looked so very old, rusty-red with time, dessicated, worn down with wind. So too its people, eyes sunk back into the skull, hair matted like tumble-weed, energy sapped by heat and drought and emptiness.

It was this world the Europeans had claimed not so long ago. It looked well enough at the coast, bountiful in its botany, but each exploration of the interior opened up more nothingness. Men starved and died with great simplicity. They set off with horses, full packs and good cheer. The Aborigines watched them on their way and then, with no interest or dismay, watched them return a few weeks later, starved of food, shrivelled, short of hope and every other need. Mount Destruction was a modest hump of land not far from the place where I had bogged the truck. To my eyes it seemed undeserving of such a name but the man who had called it that had reason. His name was Ernest Giles.

Having driven myself deeply into Australia, and having eventually extracted the machine, I felt a personal involvement with that particular place. Consequently, as soon as I learned it had also been important to an explorer operating in the area exactly 100 years beforehand, I felt a bond with him. The more I read of his accounts the more it seemed as if nothing had changed between his day and mine. I could step into his shoes without difficulty; it was all as he had left it. To imagine, say, the Portuguese vessel blown into Guanabara Bay in 1502 (which thereby initiated the city of Rio de Janeiro) is almost impossible; too much has changed. To think of Giles, while bathing in the same stretch of water that refreshed him and his horses, and listen to the galahs still calling from the trees, is to expect him, almost to see him, in that selfsame spot.

Giles was a typical immigrant. He left Bristol in England when he was 15, joined his parents who were already in the new colony and soon made his way further and further inland. There was no complexity about the man. He wanted to do well, to transform a piece of Australia into something similar to a part of Gloucestershire. Not for him any vague talk about the wonder of a wilderness. He wanted to see what the country had to offer and would then adapt such offerings into profit and a decent way of life.

In reading his journals (with their elegant prose and frequent quotations) it is easy to be attracted by his straightforwardness. To him there was no virtue in 'interminable scrubs'. He wanted water, good grazing, temperate climate, an absence of natives, and all those benefits that he had left behind securely in the hands of other, richer and landed countrymen. I personally love the simple names that all such immigrants brought from Britain and attached to the new bits of natural history that came their way. Without anything in the way of taxonomic relevance there are scrub turkeys, wild currants, desert figs, ghost gums, bulldog ants, grass trees and paddy melons. I began to call it Spitalfields English, imagining some Cockney uprooted from the East End, with few biological names to guide him but affixing them confidently whenever there seemed cause.

'What's this?' a friend might have said.

'Well,' says our Londoner, 'let's say it's a black oak. And over there's a mulga ant, and that one's a meat ant, and this one's a honeypot ant.'

And so they are called still, along with desert poplars, thorny devils, defenceless dragons, never-fail grass and dead-finish bushes.

We had with us a guide named Len, an excellent fellow who gave all these names an extra harmony by pronouncing them in a correctly Australian manner, where the vowels are all fowls—or so they sound to English ears.

'What's this?' we would ask in our quest for further names.

'Oh, that's a desert oak,' he would reply, immediately, nasally, and after the briefest of glances at a tree that was assuredly no oak. Oh, that's a mountain devil (a lizard), a black boy (a plant), a red back (a spider), a cape lilac (another tree, also called a cedar). Quite new words like spinifex were the exception. There were clumps of this everywhere and, before long, a snake was seen slithering in their midst.

'What's that?' we said, with happy anticipation.

'Oh, that! Well, we call that a spinifex snake.'

I am not certain if Len, for whom central Australia was reality and anywhere like Spitalfields as remote as Darwin, Perth or Townsville, welcomed the continuing joke, but he steadily supplied the material for it. Once the truck stopped savagely when we had run over a piece of string apparently pulling itself across the road. We stared at it in amazement. Nose to tail, it was a succession of furry, creeping grubs, the progenitors of butterflies. It was enchanting. We diverted the leader and the others obediently followed. Eventually, the long string completed its passage of the road, wound through the grass, climbed up a tree and then became a ball of writhing, looping, curling things.

'What on earth are they?' we asked.

'Oh,' said Len, 'you really don't know? Well, it's a strange name we have for them. You see out here we call them caterpillars.'

Ernest Giles's journals are similar, taking note of the blood-woods, the cypress pines, and the fact that bulldog ants were always in the shade of every desert oak. His fame as a man, and the reason for his journals, lay in his decision to be first to travel from Australia's centre to Australia's western shore. In 1874, when he set out, no one had done the trip. No one even knew what kind of country lay between the middle and the Indian Ocean edge. Giles took three companions, twenty-two horses and not much in the way of rations. He felt a confidence in Australia that had already killed other such explorers. No one would take horses across the Sahara, but then no one knew Australia.

Giles's general attitude to the wilderness (and the reason I have chosen him) was the simple doctrine that has been with mankind until the confusion of the last few years; what kind of place is this and how can use be made of it? At the conclusion of his journeying, and with the realisation that only wilderness had come his way, he was distraught and wrote a dismal epitaph. However, that lay ahead of him when he set out and came to the spot where my vehicle and I had floundered in the dark red mud. I had bathed, as I have said, in the pool where he had bathed. I had felt happy there and so had he. I had no Aborigines watching me from the nearby hills as he had, and I was to suffer no moment of fear as he did in that place. His companion Gibson, sufficiently moved by the sight of all that water, also cast off his clothes and washed. This was the first time he had done such a thing for eighteen hot and dirty weeks. A further companion saw the sight and rushed to Giles shouting out this news. Giles grabbed for his gun. He scanned the skyline. He saw the lines of spears up there on the hills—and then he learned of Gibson's bath. He laughed, rushed to see the sight, and resolved to use another pool in future. I, having immersed an equally encrusted frame into that same water, began to feel more of a bond with Gibson than with his leader. However, it was the last bath that Gibson was ever to take.

The place was an oasis. It still is. Giles knew the problem in the arid land lying to the west would be food and water. Consequently he was loath to leave the security of a spot that had shade, a short stream and various creatures (all good for the pot) coming to drink at it. Even today it is difficult to leave; the shade and the clear pools exert their magnetism. A whole century has passed but a visitor will still agree with Giles's summing up: 'It was a place I greatly liked, and it was free from ants. There was a long line of fine eucalyptus timber and an extensive piece of ground covered with rushes, which made it look very pretty; altogether it was a most desirable spot for an explorer's camp, and an excellent place for the horses, as they soon got fat here.' Giles even quoted John Bunyan: 'Methinks I am as well in this valley as I have been anywhere else in all our journey; the place methinks suits my spirit. I love to be in such places, where there is no rattling with coaches, nor rumbling with wheels.'

Me too; I agree with both of them. However, Giles was still determined to head west. He smoked a horse, by name Terrible Billy, who proved to be as terrible in death as in life, tough and intractable. He left two men behind, beneath the gums and by those pools, and set off with Gibson, four good horses, and as much water and smoked Billy as they could carry. Gibson was a strange choice, being a poor bushman, idle, careless, lean-witted and argumentative, but it was this last characteristic that won him the place. He complained that he had not been favoured with responsibility thus far and his turn had come. Giles yielded, but it was Gibson who paid the price of winning that argument.

The horses were highly relevant to Giles's hopes for the uncharted land ahead of him. He was only interested in finding fertile country and (to my mind) this made him choose such conventional transport. He was not an adventurer, wishing to pit himself against the odds that came his way. Had he been, and had he been hoping for that sort of glamour, he might have thought of camels rather than the prosaic, unheroic, everyday beasts he actually selected. There were already camels in Australia, imported from Afghanistan the moment that earlier explorers had learned about the interior of the new land, but Giles took only horses. When doing work in a hot place their consumption in gallons per hour is similar to a tank. A full, five-gallon water-bag, for example, does not last long: it is sucked dry, seemingly half a gallon at a gulp, by a single beast in a matter of moments.

Anyway, Giles set off. Fortunately, water was encountered after twenty miles at a place he called the Circus. Less fortunately, he discovered that Gibson, entrusted with packing Terrible Billy, had made the no less terrible error of including far less meat than was required. Nevertheless, and on 21 April 1874, they left the Circus on a westwards course, making forty miles on that first day. The country was undulating sandhills, speckled with spinifex and dotted with blood-wood trees. 'Its general appearance', wrote Giles, 'is by no means displeasing to the eye, though frightful to the touch.' On the second day, with the horses mopping up water as insatiably as desert sand will do, they rode another forty miles. The two pack animals, now with no water left to carry, had become a burden themselves. They were taken back along the tracks for a mile or so and thwacked in the direction of the Circus water-hole.

On 23 April Giles and Gibson with the two remaining horses travelled a further eighteen miles to the west (with several hundred still ahead of them). The journal records: 'Here Gibson, who was always behind, called out and said his horse was going to die, or knock up, which are synonymous terms in this region.' Ahead of them, some thirty miles distant, was a range of hills that they thought—erroneously—might indicate a change for the better but, with heavy hearts and on the fourth day, the two men started their retreat. Gibson's horse lasted one more mile and then fell, knocked up and put down by thirst and heat. Few exploratory expeditions in the world can have been quite so speedily overcome.

That was sadness; the rest was tragedy. Within a few miles all the water had gone. Giles's mount, the Fair Maid of Perth, was still in good shape. So Giles put Gibson on this horse instructing him to reach a cache of water they had left behind as quickly as possible. He was then to press on to the Circus, refresh both himself and the horse, ride on to collect the others, and finally return to rescue Giles. As with so many tales linked to the invasion of central Australia, such as that of Burke and Wills, there is a desperate succession of things going wrong.

Gibson set off. He reached the deposit of water. He and the mare drank some, left the rest for Giles and headed for the Circus, following the tracks made on the outward journey. Then, as now, tracks on the hard dry sand set within its sea of spinifex last for an age. Unfortunately, the two horses sent back on their own had, after a while, elected to leave the original pathway. They had chosen to travel further to the south. For some reason the wretched Gibson, floundering along with hunger, thirst and no more intellect than formerly, chose to follow the path made by the two pack-horses rather than the four sets of tracks from their outward journey.

Giles, stumbling along later on foot, drank from the cache and then came upon the dividing point. He was horrified. He could see what had happened, with Gibson's error being clearest of all. There was no point in compounding it and, at some five miles per day, half-conscious for much of the time, he limped towards the Circus. There 'Oh, how I drank! how I reeled! how hungry I was! how thankful I was that I had so far at least escaped from the jaws of that howling wilderness'. Refreshed, and more alert with water inside him, he hears a squeak by the bank of that creek. It proved to be a small and dying wallaby 'scarcely furnished yet with fur'. Giles pounced on it, eating every morsel, skin, bones, the lot. This was not Gloucestershire. This was not what he had come 10,000 miles to find.

The two men reclining beneath the gums and by the Sladen Water were horrified when their leader staggered back to camp, a ghost of his former self. Without his companion, without a single horse, and without food and water; it was just twelve days since he had set forth with fair supplies, fat horses and high hopes. This was Australia and it was a bitter disappointment. However, it was also eight days since Gibson had last been seen and, after twenty-four hours of recuperation, Giles set off with one of the other men to look for him. They reached the Circus, saw no sign, reached the dividing of the way and then followed Gibson's tracks. Unfortunately, as was soon discovered, Gibson had not even followed the other horses but had wandered off with the Fair Maid even further to the south, and therefore even further from the only known water-holes. The two men tracked him until, once again, they could go no further. Giles's journal is rich with lament: 'The mare had carried him God knows where, and we had to desist from our melancholy and unsuccessful search. Ah! who can tell his place of rest, far in the mulga's shade? or where his drooping courser, bending low, all feebly foaming fell?' Later, he called 'this terrible region that lies between the Rawlinson range and the next permanent water . . . Gibson's Desert, after his first white victim to its horrors'.

Inevitably one has questions. Giles was among the last of the major explorers of Australia and he must have known how the others had fared. His travels came after those of Grey, Mitchell, Sturt, Stuart, Eyre, Warburton, Leichhardt, Burke and Wills. None of those had had an easy time—the last three had all died—and Giles certainly knew of their exploits. In fact, he and Gibson happened to set out, and mentioned the fact to each other, on an anniversary of the Burke-Wills expedition. Therefore, was it just wishful thinking that made them act in a manner which, coupled with the desert they encountered, led to such an abrupt return? I think so.

Giles's disquiet at finding only a 'howling wilderness' was intense. I believe the wish to find areas suitable for settlement, rather than a lust for fame, was still the cause of his subsequent return to the Gibson desert. He was then better equipped, wiser and supported by camels. This time he succeeded in crossing Australia, and reached Perth before crossing back again about 400 miles north of his first traverse; but he found little to his liking in 2,500 miles of exploration. 'This was a great disappointment to me . . . It could never have entered into anyone's calculations that I should have to force my way through a region that rolls its scrub enthorned, and fearful distance out, for hundreds of leagues in billowy undulations, like the waves of a timbered sea, and that the expedition would have to bore its way, like moles in the earth, for so long, through these interminable scrubs, with nothing to view, and less to cheer.'

It is still Giles's prose, no doubt about that, but the effervescence has gone in this personal assessment of his achievements. His views on exploration make the point yet more acutely: 'Although the greatest honour is awarded and the greatest recompense given to the discoverer of the finest regions, yet it must be borne in mind, that the difficulties of traversing those regions cannot be nearly so great as those encountered by the less fortunate traveller who finds himself surrounded by heartless deserts.' How sad that he even felt it necessary to point out that an unwelcoming landscape makes life rough for its invader; but he was even more right about reward. Thomas Mitchell, for example, had a far easier time of his exploration, discovering Australia Felix (the western part of the State of Victoria) and inducing a stream of overlanders to settle there. For his labours he was knighted, he received an honorary degree from Oxford and much money from the government of New South Wales. Giles earned a gold medal from the Royal Geographical Society and nothing else. He got a job as a clerk at £150 a year and died in poverty in 1897. It would appear that his fellow countrymen agreed with him: if the explorer can find nothing useful his exploration has been at fault.

There are other questions and these relate, in large part, to the Aborigines. It must be odd, as well as insulting and sometimes fatal, having foreigners discovering your land. Giles was exploring, naming, claiming and staggering through a wilderness that was the homeland of these other people. It was the only place they knew, and the first token of impending change was the sight of men and horses passing through their territory. Either the invaders found the traditional watering holes, and carried on to the horizon, or they failed to do so and marked the spot with their bones.

Once again Giles reflects his times and not ours. His journal shows him to be sensitive, discerning and sympathetic—his occasional turns of phrase are often a delight—but for him the residents meant nothing. It is surely disagreeable having a group of local people observing you when you are gasping and crawling through a land that is quietly providing them with an adequate living. At best Giles is amicable with the natives, if pompous: 'I

Desert rivers meander as any other but are often dry as dust save for the times when, once a year or one year in ten, water hurtles down. Overleaf, wind-blown sand in northern Kenya, a rare sight in deserts. Below, a Ghost gum, cave paintings, and Parakeelya in central Australia.

showed them matches . . . ignition of some grass was too startling a phenomenon for their weak minds. I presented [the chief] with several matches . . . arranged in Nature's simple garb, he stuck them in his hair.' At worst Giles is apparently devoid of compassion for other kinds of people.

When he had gone to look for Gibson he had left one man behind. The Aborigines, seizing their chance, had advanced to investigate. Jimmy, the remaining man, then loosed off everything available and Giles's journal subsequently recorded the event: 'I gave the lad great praise for his action. He had had a most fortunate escape from most probably a cruel death, if indeed these animals would not actually have eaten him.' Perhaps he is right that young Jimmy would have been killed, and eaten. What is also right is that Giles saw the people much as he saw their wilderness. It had to be tamed and thoroughly cleared of all unpleasantness before it could be used by men rather than animals.

I read Giles's journal in a most appropriate place. Far from the rattling of coaches or the rumbling of wheels, I rested beneath the fine eucalyptus timber on soil still free from ants. It was not free from flies, alas, and it was still warm (as Giles had phrased it), substantially over 100°F; but it was the proper spot to read his words. The white bark of the ghost gums was dazzling in the sun. The galahs and budgerigars were perfect company; they shrieked and fluttered to let me know whenever a kite flew by. Giles might have left only the day before, save that I would have seen more marks of his stay—the hoof-prints, the place they built to smoke poor Billy, the spears and cartridges lying on the ground. Perhaps a greater truth is that it looked as it had done the day before Giles, his three companions and twenty horses had arrived upon the scene. It certainly had no sign of any modern thing, save me. It was unbruised, untouched and wholly marvellous, to me at least.

That, in a sense, is the trouble. An oddness of modern man is that he is so frequently just a visitor. He does not have to make a

---

'Well, we've dammed a bit of a stream, and the kids like it, and I like it, and off we go.' Aborigine children on a reserve 400 miles west of Alice Springs.

living in all the places where he spends his time. He can bring in food, or arrange for it, and does not have to see each landscape as a good or bad provider. Giles, and so many of his kind, were living from the land and hoping to do so for the rest of their days. They could not see the place any differently. I could take delight in the caddis-sticks walking in the pool, the round limbs of the well shaped gums, the redness of the rock, the ripples of the sand; but what was there to eat among that lot? At the stirring of saliva, at the hint of any appetite, I could reach across, select some morsel from a rucksack and then rest content again. What could I know of earlier feelings, however similar the place? It was the eye of the beholder that, as always, makes all the difference.

For instance, there were no spears ranged along those hills, no grizzled faces, no long black bodies, no woomeras to help them throw their weapons down at me. My first real sight of Aborigines came when a car once rattled past me along a lonely road. The vehicle itself was outstandingly noisy, an external combustion machine that should by rights have died a decade earlier; but it also poured out sound of a different kind. Only one person was in the driving seat, a white girl in a cotton dress, but every other place was full of blond-headed, brown-skinned, shouting, hooting, calling kids. More like a centipede upon its back than any car, it waved limbs from every opening. Like children anywhere, when twenty-five have packed themselves in the space for four, they made much of the consequent disorder.

'Just where were you taking that lot?' I asked that evening, when the same cotton dress swam into view. It could hardly be missed in the small community where we were staying; there were not too many of them.

'Oh, out to Amaraltji, where we've dammed a bit of a stream, and they like it, and I like it, and we get out the Chev. and off we go.'

I was out there when next they arrived. The screaming centipede hove into view and then, on stopping, became a grenade. It exploded into more than a score of independent parts and these hurtled themselves instantly towards the dammed-up pool. Without hesitation they ran into the water. A piece of tranquillity, quietly reflecting the sandstone rocks on every side, became a bubbling and a shouting and a wild whooping which was of course a joy to watch. It was also infectious. I have no tangle of sun-bleached hair, and no nut-brown body, but I did have a raggedy pair of pants, much as they all had, and I too plunged into the pool.

'Good on you,' said the girl, with just the right accent for that hallowed phrase, and a smile right for anywhere.

Later the children climbed up the rocks, lay flat on them for two seconds at a time (which is how those of their age maltreat the science of basking) and then climbed all other obstacles that came their way—trees, slopes, or more rocks. The sky became less blue as the sun slipped down, the rocks more red, the children even duskier in the dusk that fell about them. Occasionally there were some adults, with black hair, black bodies, and as still as the rocks on which they sat. To look at an elderly Aborigine face (although such a face will scarcely ever look at you) is to see something immensely old. Its eyes are almost as void as those of a skull. It is withered. It is motionless, and black. It appears to belong to quite another time.

The area in which I spent most days, and where we made our film, was an Aborigine reserve. This means that a particular region of hundreds of thousands of square miles belongs to them, whatever events subsequently come to pass. Such a gift, or rather the return of something previously taken, might seem a modest donation considering its barren properties. Ernest Giles, always trenchant in his opinions, had said 'it is so desolate that it is horrifying even to describe'. He had wanted meadows, suitable for pasture. Since then other men, who had learnt how sheep or cattle can live in such dry areas, might have been able to make a go of it; but its remoteness would always have been a difficulty. In fact, it was the great extent of this isolation, that gave it an unexpected purpose when the last major war had ended. There was at that time considerable momentum to testing and exploding things and, when it could no longer be fulfilled upon the heads of the enemy, some empty land had to be found. Where better than in south and west Australia? Britain's first atomic bomb was exploded there. And many of Britain's missiles were launched there, crashing down-range among the spinifex that Giles had hated so deeply.

When those days were over, and when days of more consideration for indigenous people had arrived, the area reverted to its original status. It became a home for Aborigines. Unfortunately, although a wilderness is swift to reclaim its former dominions, people are often less willing to do so. A life of digging up witchety grubs, skinning snakes and eating termites does not have the same appeal as formerly. The young men wander into towns. There, assisted by alcohol and welfare cheques, they can live new lives that are also without appeal. Drink has its power to exacerbate any mood, making the jolly jollier but the desperate abysmal in their despair. Over in Alice Springs, which Nevil Shute called a bonzer town, the Aborigines sit by the roadside, sleep in the dry sand of the Todd river, lurch into shops and point and grunt at the things they want to buy. In the main they are a most unbonzer addition to that unbonzer scene.

Out in the country everything—to my mind—is rather better. There are still the welfare cheques, the payments of a rich state to its former occupants, that make it possible to be extremely dissolute, if dissolution happens to attract. There are also food hand-outs, initiated in the really bad years and often maintained because the begging hands still beg even when the rains have come again. There is employment in the reserves, largely of the construction kind, and the men can then earn more money to add to their weekly cheques. They work one day, forget the next, and labour with the gaiety of undertakers. There was no banter, no chat, no sign of liveliness—at least in my presence. Perhaps that was the fault, and I was the fault; but I have sat with Bushmen, Japanese and Eskimos and never before have I felt so completely at a loss as in Australia. Those eyes were caverns and inextricably deep.

Things might have been better had I been able to bring the conversation around to motor cars. Speaking at all was difficult; hardly any white Australians speak an Aboriginal language and listening to an Aborigine attempting English does not lead to instant comprehension; but cars would have been a subject to start on. They seem to love them. Given $400 or so, they hurry off to buy another. The purchases are not tip-top but they can leave the garage and, with luck, will put quite a few miles behind them before, either pushed in despair or through mishap, they finally leave the road. There they stay. One sees more cars than Aborigines in the emptiness of their reserves. The things glisten brightly, enduringly, in just the spots where they have died. As in surgery, their parts can help to preserve the living but, unlike surgery, without a need to copy the original. I saw one car that showed a cunning no ordinary mechanic would dare to emulate. Clutches and brakes both need hydraulics, but a car's clutch is more crucial than the impediment of a brake. Therefore, should the clutch hydraulics fail, switch to the alternative and transplant the brake hydraulics in their place. The car will work again and, with none too many hills, will surely give good service until a downward slope is reached that, inexorably, builds up momentum until one more shiny shell of steel is added to the countryside. The wrecks are everywhere. They are even useful: turn right by the black Pontiac. They are also sad, and one more kind of litter in a wilderness; but cars could have made a talking-point: I feel sure of that.

However, I failed. I failed with those men squatting by the rock pool. I failed with others, sitting on the sand beneath scarecrow mulgas that did nothing to hide the sun. I would sit with the flies, looking or not looking at those sunken downcast eyes, and would let time pass as they too let it go. I would gaze at the dogs, wonder at their thinness, and question to myself why they did not even pant, or shift their position, as from time to time I was forced to do. There were tins. There was sometimes a fire, with the barest whisper of smoke curling away from it. There was occasionally a weapon, such as a spear, or the shell of a dynamo, or a bit of cloth impaled upon the tree, or just nothing, apart of course from the flies and that scarecrow shadow etched upon the sand.

I once went with a fairly ancient man (and they all seemed to be ancient the moment youth had gone) to a cave in a hill.

'We call it Cave Hill,' explained the friend named Len.

'What do *you* call it?' I asked the Aborigine, but the question was lost in the air. It evoked no answer, no glance, no sign of any kind that it had ever been put. There was another person with us, a woman who asked questions much as some simple sower might sow seeds on to rock: she would ask and ask, despite the lack of all reward. The day, therefore, held promise for beating all others in its absence of communication.

However, there was no death of pictures, the things we had come to see. Within the cave beneath the hill—Len's name had accuracy as well as brevity—every piece of wall space had been covered. There were figures, shapes, animals, formless colourings, all interspersed and interposed. The drawings were not good, in that the dogs, wallabies and people were neither clear nor impressionistic, but they were fun and bright and good to see. 'I could draw like this once,' said Picasso when opening a children's exhibition. Mankind could always draw as in Cave Hill, putting colours and lines where impulse puts them happily.

'How old are these?' said the lady. 'Wouldn't you say they were done hundreds of years ago, all on top of each other like this? And where do the colours come from? And how have they stayed so crystal clear?' She seemed to fill the musty, bat-smelling, pigeon-dropping cavern of air with an awful lot of sound. The old man did not look at her, or at the paintings, or at us, but turned his head slowly from side to side and seemingly saw nothing on the way. However, the lady refused to accept such locked-up intelligence. She placed herself in front of him. She moved her head to catch, as she hoped, his eyes and then, having gripped them with a stare, she asked straight to his face: 'Is this the place where old men brought young men to learn the ancient rituals?'

She paused. The silence was loud but the man seemed about to speak. He almost looked at her, and then he said some words. The rest of us craned to hear them, and were amazed at the sudden sentence he had hurried out. It was strung together, words into words, a blur without an edge of any kind. It took time to fathom. And then its sound struck home to me. Within that rumbling he had said, 'It's-place-where-old-men-fuck-young-girls.' At least, I think he did. Or was it me, trying to sort sense out of his sound? I

94

looked at her. I looked at Len and looked again at the Aborigine. We all ended gazing at the ground before walking from the cavern in to the bright, bright sun.

By then it was lunch-time and, clambering into the vehicle, we were soon speedily, dustily and determinedly on our way to somewhere else. By then the time had gone for clarification, and the old man's black and dusty hair lay back in the wind as we bumped and thumped along that brick-red road. I still did not know if I had heard him aright, but I do know that the lady never asked him another thing. As for Len, he was smiling, but then he always did, and he turned to look at a vast distance of flowers on my side of the vehicle.

'Oh, them . . .' he said, after I had put an eyebrow into a question mark. 'Oh, them, their proper name is poached-egg daisies, but daisies will do if you're running short of time.'

At last I was able to laugh, and so did he, very loudly, and so did the lady, just a little bit. In fact, although I was never sure of anything with the distant black-skinned man, I could almost swear there was an extra crack or two upon his ancient face.

The days in Australia were extremely happy. We flew from place to place, either high to get some feeling of its size, or low to learn its details, its kinds of tree, its contours. We drove wherever possible, wishing there were more kangaroos, looking at the buttons and everlastings (two more kinds of daisy), eating or just resting beneath the solitary shade of the umbrella mulgas, and revelling in a land more rich with vegetation than any desert but just as empty of modern man and all his works. The few cattle stations on the edge of the reserve—it was far too arid for sheep— were confusingly similar, at least to a dusty, well-worn, much-driven visitor.

First were the shiny blades of the clanking wind-wheels. then the aerials, bringing school and news and shopping lists from one remoteness to another. And finally the clutter around each home, the dead vehicles, the old iron, bits of tree, packing-cases and ancient furnishings, all picked over by the chickens, climbed over by the children, pushed over and left over from the past. No money had been lavished on the house itself; that, as like as not, was more of a shack with outhouses than a solid home. The cash had gone on the huge Mercedes truck with its several trailers in a line, on the 3,000 Hereford-Redpoll crosses wandering upwind never far from the boreholes, and on finding the water. On this bare land the essentials were all too plain.

The Gibson desert itself and the rest of the reserve was probably emptier of people than it had ever been since the black invaders from the north had first wandered that way. Giles would have been amazed, and somewhat sickened, to discover his barren land was yet more destitute; but, with white men forbidden and Aborigines moving into settlements, like Docker River, like Amata, the place is being deserted. It is so much easier for the Aborigines to have a breeze-block hut, plus a local store giving credit against those weekly welfare cheques. There is a school, a medical centre, and a garage with fuel. There are jobs at hand, if need be, and there is access to the populated areas, if they happen to attract. On the other hand the emptiness is still on every side whenever that exerts its special appeal. 'What is the main problem?' I once asked in a hospital. 'Keeping them in here long enough to cure the blighters,' said a quietly desperate man.

To walk in some wildernesses is to encounter a surprising number of people. To walk in much of the Australian outback is to know that nothing of the sort will occur. People drive, and they have horses, but long-distance pedestrians are not a feature of the land. Even the famous walkabout, when the Aborigine leaves modern trappings (including sick-beds) for something simpler, seems to be more of a driveabout or just a sitabout. Masai walk for ever, Brazilian Indians can spring from nowhere, Eskimos will appear quite suddenly far from their homes, but any abrupt meeting with an Aborigine is not a matter of seeing long black legs striding through the spinifex. It is to realise, with a sudden start, that the shade of this or that mulga tree is quietly occupied.

I walked a lot in Australia, near the weather station called Giles (a fragment of immortality for that unhappy man), near the pool at Amaraltji where the blond, bronzed children swam, and near the places where in that wet autumn the desert clogged all carelessly driven vehicles. It was quite possible to be axle-deep in mud one moment and then, a few hours later, having laboured mightily, to be axle-deep in bone-dry sand a few yards further on. In a sense this was all to the good. Such unscheduled stops were always rewarding because so much more became visible that could not be seen in the hurry of movement. An emu standing on its own. Or a wedge-tailed eagle pinpricked against the sky. Or a whole bank of parakeelya, flowering pink with fleshy leaves among the sand and tremendous compensation for anyone bothering to stretch his legs for fifty yards.

Even from Alice Springs, Australia's central outpost of a town, it was possible in a very short time to walk without the expectation of meeting another human being. Leave the hotel, find Todd Street, carry on past Traeger Park until it becomes Gap Road and then, somewhere near the junction with the Stuart Highway, start to scramble up the slope of the Macdonnell Ranges. These sound bigger than they are. They are more like a tall wrinkle stretching across the earth, as are so many ranges in this area; but in any flattish world the man who climbs up anything can feel a sort of king. I certainly liked it up there, looking far over Alice, seeing the shape of the land, sniffing the air and stumbling over rocks and plants. The going was difficult, the view superb, and what better occasion for sitting down, notebook in hand, upon a rock still warm from the middle of the day? If there had been a companion, he or she would have been subjected to a battery of random utterances. As it was, the notebook had to accept my opinions. The thoughts were spasmodic, without great connection, but they were written with feeling. Here are just a few.

There is no wrong noise in a wilderness; everything is correct.

There is privilege at seeing something that no one else can ever have seen; a group of birds, for instance, in just the right light, the right touch to the air and just the right smell.

There is no antagonism to natural obstacles, such as a stream in flood, a bush of thorns. City obstacles are man-made and antagonism there is easy.

A camera can prevent observation; it has clicked and there is no need to look any more.

Wilderness

In a wilderness it is easy to think of my stream, my bird, my place; no one else was there at the time, the experience was personal, and the possessiveness very strong.

Quietly to watch another walking through a wilderness is to note the enormous response to that single invasion, scurrying creatures, alarm calls, reaction on every side. By the same token one cannot know a thousandth part of the commotion caused by one's own presence.

We are used to living in a man-made, unnatural world; it is therefore hard to realise in a wild place that everything has a natural cause, every scattering of flowers, every shape of the land, the rock, the earth.

It is so easy to succumb to magnets, to climb Ayer's Rock, see Simpsons Gap; but there can be rich rewards in looking the other way, seeing one insect at your feet, discovering something for yourself.

If one had a wish it would be for a greater tameness of all creatures; not excessively but nearer than the skyline. Dorothy Parker was so right: 'The bird that feeds from off my palm is sleek, affectionate, and calm, but double to me is worth the thrush a-flickering in the elder-bush.'

It is fascinating how everything is invisible until it is suddenly and hugely conspicuous; a moment ago that eagle was not there, now there is nothing else in view.

It is not a matter of stopping and staring. It is of stopping and then it will happen. To sit down and do nothing is slowly to become aware of so much more, of those ants, this spider, that call, these little things.

Even to record information is to stop seeing something else. To listen for one noise is deliberately to neglect the rest. It is all so painful.

On antagonism there is every difference between a yapping city dog and a howl in the wild; it is the difference between barbed wire and a blackberry bush.

In a wilderness all senses are working, alert, active; in a city underground system, I believe that nothing is operational. It is possible to be standing next to a friend without seeing him.

Radio waves are as nothing without a receiver to collect them; a man in a wilderness has so few receivers that he misses practically everything round about him. Humility is, or will be, paramount.

Pride can also exist; the grasshopper makes use of one's shirt, a bird relaxes its alarm and settles on its eggs again. There is even a happy sense of involvement when a dung-beetle rolls away one's simple offering.

98

The pages received such reaction to the wilderness. They also became browner as hands soiled with that red countryside printed marks upon them. The sun dropped speedily down the sky and the evening grew suddenly dark. My companion, an is-bird, ceased its song (Len had said that its call, dit-dit dit-dit-dit, being the Morse for I S, gave it the title) but I neither saw the bird nor found its proper name. At all events I had to leave the rocks, the bird and the place because, in the morning, I had to leave Australia.

I got up, put away my notebook, cranked limbs into movement and decided on a longer and different way down. The sun vanished and the moon rose to guide me over the prickly, jagged countryside. I walked a long way and became splendidly tired. The solitary wrinkle of the Macdonnell Ranges seemed to go on for ever, but I had to leave it and scrambled down the hill. Suddenly, out of the darkness, there loomed a fence. It was tall and difficult. I walked along it to find a gate. That was easier, and I climbed over to see a notice on the other side. It had the belligerence of so many notice-boards. It offered all manner of punishment for climbing over that fence and for being on the land where I had walked. I have no idea why my trespass had been such a sin but I did know, sadly, that I was back in the ordinary world again. I had left the Australian wilderness. It, together with its bulldogs, paddy melons, never-fail, poached-eggs, grass trees, red backs, mountain devils and dead-finishes, was firmly at an end. I had been very happy there.

5 Mountain

Very much country, Sir.
The Sherpa Aila to Toni Hagen as both stood on a Himalayan summit

A banging door. My banging door. A shout; a call. What a time to start a day! I get up, dress, pack, pay, and doors bang behind me. The taxi arrives. Bang go its doors. Just how many times do doors slam to get two people in a car? Out through the Heavitree gap to the airport. The doors slam again, one, two, three, four for me and the driver. I check in. The case goes one way, I another. I sit down and wait, stand up and wait, walk and wait and finally climb up trembling aircraft steps. Soft music, a different smell, a clunk from the door, and then that ludicrous leap from the ground as ninety tons of cowling and spar, engine, powder-room and stewardess take to the air. Some eggs are set before me and I look at the time. It is still an early hour to start the day.

Clouds. Wonderful clouds. A horizon full of them. A wild, beautiful, unkempt world six miles below our compact community of legs, elbows, trays and drink. Then a change in noise and pressure as we fly down to Darwin. The great muddy inlets become clearer, the rows of huts called homes. Not a sign of a buffalo; nor, come to that, of a human being. Out over the sea and back again to hit the runway where the black streaks of rubber

100

are most thickly packed. Clunk and the door opens. Creak and we move ourselves. We walk. We look at the car park, the taxi rank, the warehouses, the approach road and that, so far as we are concerned who cannot leave the airport premises, is all we see of the island of a town that is the end and the start of Australia. It was hit by a tornado not long afterwards, and most of its rectangular and corrugated homes were torn up and flung elsewhere, but it could not have looked more static on the day that we landed and waited until another plane was due.

Clunk. The same mixture as before, and more disbelief as again the whole device leaps into the air. Down below it is sea this time, not land, and without the appeal for staring at its pattern all those miles beneath. Besides, the day has run a substantial course. Therefore, with little delight either inside or outside, it is easy to close one's eyes. Suddenly, as they say, it is Singapore. It is no suddenness so far as the body is concerned, with its awareness of hours passed in semi-sleep; but the ending arrives abruptly. Fewer swamps this time, and a natural harbour growing more unnatural every frenzied day. The door opens to let in heat again. It is dark and the taxi sets out to dazzle every competitor along the route. Far too swiftly there is a hotel, with soft lights, doe-eyed maidens of extreme grace, and an unbelievable view over that extraordinary harbour. Later, at a restaurant which has taken over a street, it is American sailors and scores more girls, black-booted, tight-bottomed and as busy as bees among the crowd.

More banging, more shouts. What an hour to start another day! Pack. Check out. Check in. A door. A room. A bus. A plane. Music and that smell again. The girls are Thai this time, splendidly aloof and rude. Up and then down to thump on the tyre-tracked tarmac. A bus. A carnival of an airport lounge. And then a taxi, set about with flowers and the same fierce struggle into town. It is Bangkok and dark again. Another hotel. The lift attendant offers girls. He becomes the baggage porter and keeps up his offerings. The door is closed on him but he reappears from some other entrance until that too is fastened. A different view, but the same white lights and heavy heat. The bed beckons. So does the purveyor of nut-brown flesh from beyond the door. He

101

shouts. You shout. Everybody shouts. And then, with scarce a moment's interlude, there is a different cry, the 6 a.m. alarm as another day comes before its time.

A tired taxi, weary from the night. An empty road. An airport with every occupant gathered at one end. A lonely, white-shirted, dark-trousered, black-eyed clerk, filling in boarding cards as fast as the wind but not fast enough for the hustling throng filling up his area. At last one has a card, a permit to wait in another place for another length of time. A door, a bus, more steps and then another seat of the same old kind. Perhaps there is music, perhaps a different smell, but who cares? Clonk goes the door. There is coffee, and green land beneath; a tray with its attendant smile; then nothing until a change of note and another wince as the wheels once more put black streaks upon the ground. A door, the steps, a bus, the officials, a rubber stamp, the crowds, a taxi, the hotel, a porter, a room, a bed, a slumping, and suddenly one mynah bird upon the window-sill with a view behind of splendid hills and a sprightly feeling to the air that is quite delectable. At last, at last, the journey has been ended. This is Kathmandu. And those are the Himalayas. What infinite and total joy—at last.

Not too far away is Sagamartha, as the Nepalese insist, or Chomolungma, as the Tibetans say, or Everest, as others call the highest mountain in the world. Very far away are the two ends of the colossal mountain range that everyone calls the Himalayas, after the Sanskrit name for Snow-home. Like Brazil or Antarctica, the Himalayas invite superlatives. The range is very high, with all the 8,000-metre peaks in the world rising somewhere along its length. It is very sudden and steep, having the steepest gorges of any mountain range. Above all it is vast, being the biggest of all mountain chains. On the map the true Himalayas run for 1,200 miles between the Indus river and the Brahmaputra in the east; but west of the Indus is the Karakoram, and then the Hindu Kush, and then the Pamir, and finally the Caucasus. To the east, and also given separate names despite their contiguous link with the central belt, are the high mountains of northern Burma and all the other peaks that reach through Indochina into southern China. The length, therefore, of the world's biggest mountain

102

range, which first began to heave itself up about 35 million years ago, is over 3,000 miles. That, in other places, is the distance from New York to San Francisco, Rome to the Equator, London to Tehran. Unlike the Andes, slender as a spine, the Himalayas are also fat. The high tablelands of Tibet, no less a part of the chain, have a mean altitude of 14,000 feet. Only the highest peaks in the European Alps exceed that Tibetan average.

Having leap-frogged the world, either firmly on earth or in the air, I was suddenly in a mountain kingdom. Or rather in the lazy, sultry, trim and leafy gardens of the Hotel Shanker. The city of Kathmandu, set at 4,000 feet among the giants on every side, has seldom known frost or snow. Until the end of the last war it also knew little about the world beyond the peaks, for visitors were unwelcome and the ancient barrier fulfilled its ancient role of keeping outsiders out. Today it is a place almost of pilgrimage, notably for the rich young decked in cheap cloth, armed only with travellers' cheques, pedalling or sandalling most energetically, and nearly monk-like in their devotion to the simple life until, with their one-month visa at an end, they jet to somewhere else.

Kathmandu is also narrow streets, pigeon-holed with minute shops in which men sit surrounded, at arm's reach, by all their offerings. It is wooden carvings, jutting out like poop-decks or framing windows most indulgently. It is splendid faces, eyes narrowed, from the north, or wide and round from India. It is also quite the most horrendous place for banks and banking; the act of exchanging paper of one sort into paper money becomes a gross confusion, and makes the air smell very sweet once the task has been concluded. Besides, who can fret for long when, at eye-level above the counter selling rum, there is a swallow's nest not a peck away from one's own protruding nose? I ate Chik Chow at the Om, bought umbrellas to keep off the sun, drank mineral water from bottles with marbles instead of caps or corks, and then rattled back to base in the universal taxi, all hung about with plastic botany, short on the essentials but lavish with extras, like furry steering-wheels, saintly photos and wallpaper upon the doors.

The primary purpose, once again, was to make a film. I have not digressed beforehand about this occupation, partly because it is a business securely within itself. In each wilderness there was the wish to see and then, having seen, there was the need to record the little that was possible on film. To see a desert stretching for 360°, to smell it, feel it, hear it, and then to put one rectangle of all that expanse through a camera is to know how much is not being seen. Poetry, said Robert Graves, is what is lost in translation. A travel documentary is also a diminutive part of the whole it is trying to convey. The gap is fearful. It is the price to be paid for being in such a place, for the privilege of having to describe a wonder, however modestly.

The price I personally had to pay during the wilderness tour was in speaking at the lens. It is bizarre standing or sitting in some place, working out something to say and then saying it at a piece of glass. Often, if the camera is directly before you, there is nothing to be seen in that glass but your own reflection. The chatting is therefore most ludicrous, but you are kept going by the greater oddity of the film crew themselves. The cameraman is squinting through his machine. The sound-recordist is elsewhere, usually less comfortably, and pushing his microphone as near the speaker as the cameraman's framing will permit. The producer has less to do at this time, but will wave frantically if he wishes a bird to leave a tree or a person half a mile away to hurry out of shot. Others may be holding branches to dapple the sun and any passers-by will, almost certainly, stare fixedly at the wretched speaker going through his piece. Whatever else happens, and something always does, he must carry on his quiet, sensitive, intimate chat in his own dotty looking-glass world as if he is alone within that wilderness. They say it will look well in a million living-rooms later on. So he tries to do what they say, spouting his spiel until they cry 'cut' and smile to ask for it all again.

In one sense mountaineers have done a disservice to the mountains. By concentrating on the peaks they have made us forget the variety, beauty and extent of the lower areas. A walk in the Himalayas has so much to offer, such as its people, their terracing, the bridges and views, the plants and animals, like the langur monkeys and primulas overleaf.

One further price was the weight of equipment attached to every filming foray into anywhere. There were fourteen specifically filmic items of baggage that accompanied us, some heavy as lead, such as the stock, others irritating in their shape, like the tripod. It was easy to resent them all. Part of my job was to wander off the track and discover some sight that might otherwise have stayed unseen. So I would find a flower, gentle in its isolation, and report back. The baggage train would move into action. Boxes would be lifted and wrenched up the slope. There would be people, many people. The single bloom would be surrounded by contents disgorged, by things from boxes within boxes, by clapper boards and reflector boards, by macro bits for the micro work, by accessories only needed once in every hundred shots. Eventually the plant would be left, trampled round by feet and securely trapped on film.

The necessities of film making reached an apogee in the Himalayas. Into the hotel garden one day there came two men. Their faces were like leather boots. Their actual boots were of rubber and their physical bodies were a mixture of the two, leather and rubber combined. The more I saw of them in the future the more convinced I was of that original analysis. However, on that first day, the men had come to discuss our baggage needs. We produced the film gear. We also produced a lesser pile of personal possessions, clothes for the heat and clothes for the snow-line three miles farther up. The organisation catering for our other needs supplied lists of tents and food, cooking gear and fuel, and we became increasingly enmeshed in a spiral of necessities. To take, say, fourteen items of film equipment demands eight people to carry it. And that means three more people to carry their food. And then three more people to carry tents for the eleven people already listed. And that means more food for them, and more cooking pots, and more tents, and then there was our mountain gear, and a medical box, and the arithmetic became one of those

---

A mere pedestrian can reach 16,000 feet or so in Nepal—but he will be a far fitter pedestrian at the walk's end.

exponential curves that never touch base. Where would it end? I myself like simple walking, when a modest rucksack will cope with every requirement, but the two men eventually rose from their chairs having agreed to provide a cohort to take us to the hills. There were to be six of us and thirty-four of them and that was how we finally set off. It was ludicrous, I thought, as I watched our mustering; but then I did not know a row of beans about the Himalayas.

Two days later I also could not understand what, earlier in my life, I had thought to be exhaustion. Our destination was Kalikatang, so they had said, wherever that might be, but I could not believe any goal could be worth the labour involved. Firstly, it was hot, tremendously so. Secondly, the path was often out-rageously steep, causing alarm that one might even roll to the bottom again. Thirdly, there were the porters. They were often, quite literally, half my size and would be carrying 70 lb upon their backs. They did not always resemble those two men we had met in Kathmandu who were their leaders; often they had broomstick legs, mere bones with only skin to cover them. Where was their muscle and, come to that, where were their shoes? I wore socks and plimsolls, a necessary protection against the rock from which the path was made. They wore feet and that was all. I came to believe we were two species; one a hot, flaccid lump of lard, suffering from the weight of a notebook, a camera and accumulated sloth; the other a body fixed together with sinew, scarcely visible beneath its pack, and not even perspiring as far as I could see. I was lurching, slumping and panting as if the end of life was near.

However, as I tottered into Kalikatang, lifting each foot no more than a millimetre above the ground, I saw the tents already sited. The nimble, broom-legged ones had got there first. One of them indicated an open flap and through this I flopped, finding foam rubber, a sleeping-bag and all my things within. I lay still, and slowly the earth was spinning more securely on its axis. The flap opened again and a man said 'Tea, sir' before leaving a tray near my feet. Having planned moves much as a fat man plots actions when his pen, say, has fallen to the floor, I soon had that cup of tea securely in my hand. Life returned, rather than survival.

106

Within the hour I was ready to walk again—an ability I thought had probably gone for good.

Life returned, and so did joy. The tents were all within a grove of long-needled pines. The ground sloped away on every side, a sequence of terraces of unbelievable beauty. Of course the landscape was irregular but almost every part of it had been fashioned into staircase terracing. Unlike fields, which roll with the land itself, the terraces were angled to it. Their sharpnesses emphasised the shape beneath, much as mosaic does when its fragments of straightness flow round an architrave. The crop was barley, in the main, and at its greenest. Man had laboured tremendously—just think of all that work!—and the ground had been bountiful in its return.

Man! In fact, mainly one saw children and women. The children were the easiest to see because, given half a chance, they would let their curiosity overcome them, peer through tent flaps, inspect ablutions, misinterpret—or possibly interpet—solitary and pur-posive walks for temporary solitude near to camp. They wore, in general, a thick but oh-so-patched knee-length coat, folded over at the front in the manner of a dressing-gown. On their heads they had round, flat-topped hats of the same patchwork material. Below their knees and on their feet they wore nothing. Occasionally, they had some saffron rice glued, I know not how, to the centre of their foreheads. Not unreasonably, they looked grubby. Those with malformations, either of mind or body, looked grubbier; but, despite this outside poverty, they were rich company and I spent many hours with them. They did not mind, without a speck of a language between us, joining in some idle game, teasing ants from their path, tossing stones on to a stump. There are times when children—most of them—are perfect company. As when one is tired after a day's long walk. Or a view is perfection and one wishes only to sit and look at it, place sticks for ants to clamber over, flick stones towards a hollow in a tree.

Dotted among the terraces and ranged along the paths were villages. These too were built on a slope and angled like the fields on every side. They changed with altitude, being of adobe lower down and of stone and board higher up, with rocks on the roofs to keep everything in place. On the valley's other side each village resembled an eyrie, perched on nothing that one could see to account for its existence. On one's own side they were not separate entities from the fields and rocks because there were fields within them, wherever space permitted, and the rocks from which they had been built were the rocks from which the hillsides had been made. For equal harmony between man and the place he worked it would be hard to find a rival situation.

It took me quite a while to realise a stark simplicity: everything to be moved in that area always had to travel upon someone's back. In the two days since leaving the road we saw nothing wider than a mountain pathway. We had seen no horses, no wheeled vehicles. On the other hand we had seen plenty of people carrying things—firewood down from the trees, baskets of fodder for the animals, corn tied up in bundles, salt, possessions such as pots and pans—and it was all on someone's back. We had not passed a single human soul on the track not burdened down with something. Moreover, we had not been on some offshoot of a path, where life would be more primitive, but on one of the major highways that lead, and have led throughout history, from Nepal into Tibet. The smooth stones, sparkling as if mica were embedded in them, had been worn down solely by feet, by centuries and centuries of feet.

Before exhaustion had set in to kill appreciation, I had been delighted by this high road of a pathway. It was about 5 feet wide, well maintained by the local authority, the panchayat, and fulfilling a role today unchanged from its status in the past. It did not have the litter of a city thoroughfare; there were no broken bottles or jagged cans. The fragments that had fallen, God knows when, did not jar: small bits of cloth, some slivers of bamboo, a bone, a piece of brick from somewhere else. Occasionally the stones were spotted with lumps, like a pox upon the rock, and these were garnets, a suitable kind of excellence for such a perfect road. Ivan Illich has said that nothing bulldozed or machined into shape can ever have the beauty of a hand-made, man-made thing. He would be happy upon a Himalayan pathway, first chivvied into shape by feet, then fashioned where need be with steps and minor walls, and then smoothed and smoothed again by people and nothing more.

I had wondered about those walls; there did not always seem to be a real need for them. And then, at the very first resting place, I understood. If you have 70 lb upon your back, all carefully strung together, you do not or cannot off-load that pack without considerable strain. All you wish to off-load is its weight and this the wall will help you to achieve. It takes your pack from you and lets your legs stretch out. Therefore, the tops of those walls were smooth, as well they might be after packs had been rested upon them over the centuries by generations of exhausted carriers.

This talk about people, loads, highways, houses, crops and terracing might imply, as it suddenly implied to me, that the place is not a wilderness. Had I come several thousand miles, full of curiosity about this biggest mountain massif, to discover that it was not wild but had been tamed by enormous industry into a well populated zone? In a sense yes, but, in a more important sense, it was a wilderness, however occupied. With each further day's walking, my body growing increasingly capable as muscles recollected their proper function, I would be one whole day farther from roads and motor cars, electricity and normal life. It was not a matter of miles distant, as these are irrelevant when the contours of the land count for rather more. It was just a matter of foot-days. I love to hear that somewhere is a week away, or a whole moon distant, or will take the time that the sun also takes from its zenith to its setting later on. It sounds so correct. Along that Himalayan path, hearing every noise, watching every lammergeier coast from peak to peak, and surrounded by smells that changed with every shift in altitude, the visitor knows there is a gulf between this world and his own. By comparison, if by nothing more, it is a wilderness.

That may sound nonsense, and tendentious nonsense at that. If so, I am failing, because following each day's travel I was increasingly in a wilderness form of life. This struck me most in the villages. The main road, of course, went straight through them. The visitor therefore had opportunity to see more of the people, to pause—only too willingly—for gulps of breath, to look at everything there is to see, while the people, no less readily have a look at the puffing, pink-faced visitor. 'Namasté,' he says. 'Namasté,' they say in return. He feels like a dervish about to sell prophecies in, say, Iran. Or an Italian with a performing monkey in Victorian England. Or a travelling medicine-man anywhere, ready to show and sell and promise health to all prepared to buy. The arrival of a visitor was firmly part of an ancient ritual. I felt the villages were more akin to medieval Europe than anything I had ever seen even in the most medieval parts of that continent today. The beasts were intermingled with the people; cows, geese and goats below; people, in general, up above with a ladder more than a staircase connecting to the ground. Chickens, of course, were everywhere but so was smoke, oozing gently from each room, hanging low over the rooftops and entirely dominant. If there is one major change between then and now, it is that we no longer smell of smoke.

With each day's travel, further on the road towards Tibet and away from Kathmandu, there was also an accumulated increase in altitude but, above all, a steady sensation of increasing wilderness. The actual number of days of travel back to the road was critical. More than any other attribute of civilisation the road became, for me increasingly, a symbol of man's conquest of wild places. It is the roads that are opening up Brazil. It is the fact that only two places in the United States, both in the far west, are more than ten miles from a motorable track that is so significant. In England and Wales there are no more than a few spots more than two miles from a tarred road. In Scotland, wilder by far but still no wilderness, there are substantial areas of quite a few square miles at a time that are more than five miles from a tarred road. However, five miles can be walked even over the most disruptive of peat-hagged and heathered countryside in two or three hours. In the Himalayas there were soon days behind us. I and the thirty-four broomsticked, leather-hided, rubber-muscled, bare-footed file of men relentlessly put more and more of them between us and the road where our journey had properly begun. Gradually we were walking into wilderness.

110

By no means was the advance steadily uphill. 'It's all uphill except when it's down,' someone had said beforehand, and the bite of those words sunk into me when I first experienced their meaning. To labour up some tortuous stretch and then to be confronted by an identical descent can be heart-rending. Nevertheless, the business of walking along the side of a valley did mean encountering innumerable minor valleys leading into it. At the end of a hard day's stroll, after slumping into the tent, welcoming the tray of tea and recovering some energy, it could be galling to seek out the altimeter, and discover that this camp was actually lower than its predecessor a full day's march away. That, however, was also a blessing. The journey was not a matter of attaining some summit; it was to remove oneself from the road and the tamed world it entailed. The increasing distance even led to a kind of anxiety; just what would happen if real illness were to strike? The worry accentuated this particular style of incursion into the wilderness. Everything else was becoming a long way distant by the only yardstick that counted, the pace of human feet.

There was a further crucial distinction to this mountain wilderness. Nepal is a small country, being only 54,000 square miles in area (less than the size of England and Wales, the same as Czechoslovakia), but it contains almost all the climatic zones in the world. Kathmandu, as I have said, has scarcely known snow. It is on the same latitude as Florida and the Canary Islands, and only 4,000 feet above the sea. No wonder it is hot and semitropical. About three miles higher up, and not too far away, is the permanent snow-line. There the soil temperature never rises above that of freezing and biological activity is, to all intents, precisely nil. Consequently, it is possible to move from tropical to arctic conditions in a very short distance. In fact, 1,000 feet upwards (not too fearful a prospect even for city legs) is equivalent to 280 miles between the latitudes (a considerable journey for anyone). This sudden power of being able to change one's climate is found on every mountainside, where less than four feet upwards equals one mile towards the pole, but in the Himalayas it is simply more extreme. A man becomes a kind of giant who can leap in any direction, hurtle from bamboo to rhododendron in a trice, make snowmen and then, by bounding down a bit, make camp in sultry warmth.

It is all so abrupt. It is also made much more confusing by the presence not just of exotic plants and creatures, which might be expected in this place, but of very normal plants and animals that are a part of home. Around 8,000 feet there is a flourish of bamboo, geraniums, dandelions, mustard and violets—all wild by the pathside. Occasionally there are also great swathes of the pot, the hash, the plant that some still call marijuana. Above it, and looking far more alien, might be one of those trees whose flowers, large and gaudy, appear each season long before the leaves have sprouted, such as Bauhinia and Bombax. There could be coal tits, not rare for Europeans, alongside an exotic species like the orange-barred leaf warbler. There could be fantastic orchids hanging over rock, such as the *Coelogyne* white orchid, and perhaps it grows beneath the transparent delicacy of a Himalayan maple in full and gentle leaf. There could be gentians, and a normal-looking oak, and viburnum, and pieris, and overhead an Indian serpent eagle flying magnificently, piping its odd little tune. It was all so strange and contrary. As if in confirmation of this conflict a man would pass by, looking like a renegade from the army of Genghis Khan, with a near-black face and slits for eyes, and at that moment a cuckoo would start to fill the air with a feel of drowsy English summertime. Just where was I?

Well, I was about thirty miles from Kathmandu, on the eastern side of the Trisuli river, past Bakajhunda and on the way to Bhargu. Ahead in the Ganesh Himal was the Mailung valley, west of the famous Langtang, and there I would find Paldor, just a few miles short of the Tibetan frontier. That, for the time being, was the destination. If the names baffle rather than elucidate, so much the better. I was seeing the Himalayas; and whether it was the Bhote Kosi, the Trisuli Khola or any other river flowing through that heaped-up world beyond the Gosainkund Lekh, is largely irrelevant. It was strange that a Mongol warrior should walk by to the strains of the European cuckoo but the combination could have appeared, or so I was informed, anywhere along that mountain chain. So where was I? I was in the Himalayas.

At times, and when the cloud came down, it was almost necessary to say this to oneself. The mountains disappeared. The air was heavy with damp. The rhododendrons on every side looked as wet as they can do in other countries where, having been transplanted, they find the chilly moisture that always welcomes them. Lower down each Himalayan valley is *barbetum*, the sort with the scarlet flowers and smooth peeling bark. There is also *arborium*, the tallest, with red flowers at the lower altitudes, pink around 9,000 feet, and white above 10,000. No one knows why Nepal's national flower changes in this manner. Above 10,000 feet the predominant rhododendron is probably *companulatum*, still like a tree but smaller and with suede-like undersides to its leaves. In the morning, when the sun is bright, such flowers sprinkle the woods or, closer at hand, provide a gorgeous daub of colour to compare with the greens and browns on every other side. By midday in that spring season of the year, the sun has gone, lost first intermittently beyond the racing clouds that leap across the peaks and then vanished behind the more stolid damp that settles everywhere.

It is difficult to know when best to visit the Himalayas. The flowers are undoubtedly at their prime after the monsoon has come in the middle of the year. The rain brings them out and, for good measure, brings out leeches to keep them company. The days can be spiritually uplifting but physically difficult, with everything rained upon, nothing having time to dry and each leech in the neighbourhood having full opportunity to climb over socks, into boots and firmly on to feet. For some people the sight of a thousand primulas, wedged beneath rocks ensconced in trees or peppered over open places, does not compensate sufficiently for the presence of one leech, three centimetres long, swollen black with blood upon a bleeding foot, let alone dozens of them feeding in their own distinctive fashion. To travel later, and during the northern hemisphere's winter, is to find less life and also to be chilled oneself. A compromise is springtime. The rains have not come, the peaks are visible at least for half the day, the flowers are beginning, the leeches have not begun, and spring was the time that we—the six plus thirty-four of us—had started on our walk.

The days began early. At 6 a.m., encased grub-like in a sleeping-bag but well aware of cold, one realised that day had dawned. The porters, less pampered by far and presumably aware of cold (although many had brought only a shirt and shorts for the journey), were full of chat and encouraging the fires. The Sherpas, who do not carry a porter's load but administer the camp, were more functionally busy, with food, hot water and preparations for the day. One got up; or rather, as sleeping-bags demand, one got along and out and then stood up. Regret at leaving the warm cocoon was considerable but subsequent regret, on realising what wonders had already been missed, was far greater. There was perfection in each early day, silent, clean and magical. The sky had not the wisp of a cloud in it, the air no breath of movement. Smoke from our fires went up most vertically. It was an exquisite hour, still cold but with infinite promise of warmth and further glory to come.

Breakfast was brief—something hot to drink and a few biscuits for chattering teeth to bite at. There was an urgency to move, to see more before the wonder of the day had gone, and reward was always swift. A fire-tailed sunbird, with its curved beak and a dangling glory of a tail. A thick forest of enormous hemlock trees, having the dignity of redwoods and vying with the silver firs for height and width and space. There were woodpeckers, hammering away. There were bushes, hung with *Usnea* lichens as if with cobwebs. There were trees so encased with moss that they had no bark to show, and always there were plants to find, meconopsis poppies holding great globules of dew, the mandragons, saussureas, fritillaries and golden edelweiss.

Lunch appeared at about 10.30. What with filming, and diversions here and there, quite apart from deliberate dallying to give them half a chance, the Sherpas would catch up with us. They had had to wait until the moisture had left the tents, and that unnecessary extra weight had been evaporated, before packing up camp, allocating loads to the appropriate porters and then hurrying after us with the wherewithal for the next meal. Out of the most unpromising bundles would come grapefruit juice (pure nectar when the day had been hot), eggs and sausages, and baked beans far from home. When sitting on a bank of primulas, dappled by sunlight shining through the fronds above, and staring across to sharp white peaks of 25,000 feet or so, the Himalayan traveller can feel very contented with his lot. He downs the grape-fruit juice, relishes the beans and is amazed how well mere sausages can taste. Perhaps the traveller has lost his sense of judgement; but he has cause. The view, the setting, the backdrop and the prospects yet to come are excuse enough. Their excellence is sufficient to unhinge any man. Besides, a meal is always better when longed for long before its time.

The day then changed. We would continue to walk but the valleys filled rapidly with cloud. The heat vanished and backpacks that had been loaded with discarded sweaters had to disgorge them once again. The clothing helped, but the cold triumphed rapidly. It caused limbs to stiffen and relatively goat-like leapings became a thing of the past. The walk became more of a trudge and even more so when the rain began to fall. Sometimes it was heavy, and sometimes so light that it scarcely fell and merely stayed in the air until a body blundered into it. At all such times it was very wettening. The resinous litter of the pine forest mopped up the water but squeezed it forth at each imprint of a foot. The paths became rivulets. The branches above waited for their moments to drench the passer-by. This was before the monsoons were due and all the guidebooks talk insistently about the drought of spring.

'I'm glad we came in the dry season,' says a hunched-up figure sloshing in front of you. Someone answers him, but he and you and everyone else are concentrating, through battered eyelids and encircling mist, upon the one thought that is paramount: just where and when will the next campsite be?

The first sight was usually of a Sherpa, one of those who had looked so out of place upon the soft chairs of the hotel, standing with arms folded and watching as we climbed slowly up the path. Behind him was the magic of that line of tents, flaming fires by which and over which to dry and scorch one's clothes, and hot water ready for its vital transmutation into tea. Before long the sanctuary of a tent had proved irresistible. Within it was warmth and dryness. There, as we had said to each other before retiring, we would write up our notes. This could mean actually writing them, or picking up a paperback or, most likely, simply lying there, listening to the sounds outside, revelling in horizontality, remembering the walk and wishing that such a dampening was not part and parcel of every springtime day. The Himalayas are the largest mountain range and they emphasise the point repeatedly by catching every scrap of moisture that comes their way and pouring it on the heads of those below.

The first really distinctive difference in the scene comes with the ending of the forest zone. Until then the changes have been insidious; it is difficult to notice the quiet lack of something that had flourished previously. Where have all the daisies gone, and the warblers and the hemp? It requires mental labour to think back, to remember what used to be and is no more. It is always easier to notice the first of anything than the last. No one writes to newspapers, as they do in England about the harbingers of spring, to say when those welcome arrivals have finally gone, the last cuckoo of the year. However, it was not difficult to notice the end of the trees. On our path leading to the Mailung Khola they just ended. There was no falling off, no tapering with trees of smaller and smaller substance. The hemlocks either grew, and grew splendidly, or they did not. As with the firm lines on the botanical maps we passed abruptly from 'rainy subalpine forest' to 'wet alpine scrub and meadows'; and that was that.

It was also the end of people. There are few villages above 10,000 feet, although that is quite a height in itself. It is more than double the altitude of anywhere in Britain and far higher than everywhere in Australia. Some settlements exist around Dhaulagiri at 14,000 feet, but these are exceptional. Generally, above 10,000 feet it is difficult to grow crops, the actual limit fluctuating because each side of a valley receives different rainfall and differing hours of sunshine. There may still be grazing for animals within the woods; but, from a 10,000-foot base, it is simple to move the beasts, notably the goats, higher up the slope in summertime. There, within the trees, and using temporary shelter, the goatherds can watch their beloved creatures doing

116

their best to destroy yet another habitat. Of course goats feed
people, and can nibble a living where others fail and die; but it is
tempting to wish that *Capra hircus*, the Attila of conservation, the
snapper up of every vegetative trifle, the scourge of struggling,
growing things, would quietly go away. Goats can find much to
eat within an active forest, however much they may be killing
regeneration and mortally wounding the forest itself; but, fortunately, they do less well on the wet alpine scrub above the tree
line. Therefore, leaving the trees means leaving people and their
goats behind and entering a lonelier part of the enormous
mountain wilderness. Along the path we took it was then a couple
of weeks from the road—by foot.

The forests have all stopped by 12,000 feet. Thereafter the kind
of walking is completely different. Instead of seeing no more
ahead than the next big tree the view is infinitely open. The sky
can dominate once again; so too the valley's other side. Ahead the
path is visible, not for a few yards, but for a couple of thousand
feet of altitude. It winds its way up lengthily, tortuously and, if it
is steep, depressingly. The intersecting valleys are now less
frequent, but more savage when they come—a very sharp drop
down to a torrent of a stream and then a sharper rise upon the
other side. If there is wind, it can blow most violently.

Also, as we realised only too well, the thinner air was having its
effect. No longer were conversations the free and easy banter they
had been. There had to be great purpose in words to justify their
use. They interrupted the breathing flow, demanded a change in
the rhythm, made great gulps of air necessary, and were seldom
worth their utterance, however urgent the message had seemed
beforehand. The answers, if answers came at all, also took time to
come. The answerer would ponder, pumping, thumping draughts
of air.

'What's that?' says one.

'Juniper,' says another, almost monosyllabically.

'Look,' the first would say, some five minutes further on.

'What?' would say his friend, many moments later.

'Gentian.' Pause.

'Gosh.'

In this fulsome style the walk proceeded. The porters had stopped their long-range conversations. There were no girls to flirt with, perched high above the path collecting fodder, as securely out of reach as chamois, and invisible until they catcalled down to us. An occasional hunter would pass by but he, even if going downhill, would give more of a grunt than a namasté. He was lucky if he received more than a glance from any of the panting, head down, single file of men. There were still plants, like polygonum, like lychnis, and there was grass; but increasingly there was rock, either loose as scree or still firmly part of the mountainside. One welcome break was a whole field of dwarf rhododendrons. It was strange to be towering over them. Down in the woods they had grown tall, sixty feet or more, but here was the same shrub shrunk to knee-height and below. The walker had become a giant, but if he lay down and peered through the bushes he could see them in their normal scale.

Camp at these alpine altitudes was also different. Gone were the blazing logs, the splendid squandering of fuel. Gone was anything much to burn and warmth was now man-made, both in the sense of sitting communally and doing so around a flame of paraffin. Food was different. The temperature of boiling water at altitude being substantially below normal means that carrots, lentils and the like will not soften sufficiently however long they boil. Tea or coffee is less hot and, aided by a desire for internal heat, can be drunk almost the moment it is made. We sat in great duvets, ate more and retired much earlier. The sleeping-bag beckoned, despite its distance from the warmth of the eating tent, but it did not pay to leap at it too energetically. In that thin air, until we were acclimatised, all sudden effort was instantly punished by a piercing headache pain. Then, if we stood still, we could feel it seep away almost as suddenly. Some of us were lucky in this respect. I was one of them and maddeningly reminded the others frequently of this happy fact.

Eventually, on the edge of what horticulturalists often call the arctic desert, we made out highest camp. The actual tents were pitched on the crumbling, rocky earth; but all about was snow. The altitude was some three miles above the sea, Tibet was just over the skyline, Mount Paldor looked down from 19,000 feet whenever the clouds relented and a superb, unnamed, fat pinnacle of rock dominated this splendid stretch of land. There were moraines everywhere, showing clearly where glaciers had been. There were a few birds, such as grandalas hopping about starling-like on the ground. There were crows; perhaps there always are. And up above, if you stared hard a mote of an eagle would swim into your eye, going who knows where, disdainful of mere mountains down below.

'It's a Superb Eagle,' someone said, with better eyesight and knowledge than I have ever had, and I was happy to agree.

From this camp we made forays, inevitably upwards as going down could wait for our return. It was no longer walking country, not as I understand the term. An ice-axe was essential; so were glasses against the glare, and correct clothes, and sufficient respect for the lurking powers of snow. We kicked steps, took careful note of the lie of the land, and reached ridges where we could see even higher bits of rock. Save for the few people who actually climb Himalayan peaks, and then only for a few moments, there always is higher ground to gaze and ponder at.

I could see that the peaks do have appeal. They stand there insolently, like a pugilist daring another to attack. They have their defences—of cliffs, rocks and chilling temperature—and these are all in place waiting for the climber to make his move. There is a kind of bargain; the mountain cannot add to its attributes, but may unleash a few temporary extras from time to time—an avalanche, a fearful wind. The climber will also stick to the aids he brought with him, the ropes and pegs and oxygen, and will not summon up any outrageous extra of technology, thereby unbalancing the contest.

Only in 1852 did someone realise that Everest was the highest peak of all. It was discovered to be so, not in the midst of an exploration, but quietly as results came in from triangulation reports in a survey of all India. The tallest peaks were given their correct altitudes and it so happened that the 'Goddess Mother of the World', as they had called Mount Everest in Nepal, was found to be the tallest. However, it was not until 1950 that anyone succeeded in climbing a peak of over 8,000 metres. The French were the first to achieve this distinction by reaching the top of Annapurna, the 'Dispenser of Food'. Three years later, just 101 years after it had first been identified, Everest was conquered. A British expedition put a New Zealander and a Nepalese on top and the Third Pole, as some have called it, was finally won. There are now some twenty Himalayan mountaineering expeditions a year in Nepal alone, often half of them being Japanese. There are fixed fees for attempts on all major peaks and currently, so they say, mountaineering garbage is a predominant feature of each important route. Fortunately, that does not matter too much for the rest of us and, as in Antarctica, the snow and ice must do its best to bury the stuff.

Had anyone been ready to climb peaks 600,000 years ago, the highest, so it is thought, would not have been in the Himalayas. This newest mountain range, newer even than the European Alps, is still pushing up and has only achieved its eminence fairly recently. Even so, in human terms, it has been a formidable barrier for a long time. Racially the people are different on both sides, being Mongol in the north and Indo-European in the south. The religions are different, basically Hindu to the south and Buddhist to the north. Not only does virtually all the rain fall on the southern slopes but the rain shadow on the northern side is sufficient to create large deserts, which add to the barrier of the hills themselves.

Not so long ago the Himalayas were buttressed on the north by the Pleistocene ice-sheet. When that retreated, and left the Asian land mass for life to reinvade, the barrier came into its own. Creatures that could not fly or swim, cross deserts or mountaineer could only slip round by the coast of China or cross the few forbidding passes. Shivering in our tents, finding water-bottles frozen every morning, and knowing that the passes lay higher still, we found it easy to appreciate the tremendous impediment to living things that the Himalayas constitute. What warmth-loving, low-lying creatures of any kind would not have turned back long before reaching our frozen altitude? The animals that can scorn this chilling barricade are obviously exceptional, like the snow leopard, the yak, and the bhahral or blue sheep. About a hundred species of bird migrate from north to south across the Himalayas at the approach of each northern winter. Most slink through the passes, keeping as close to ground and warmth as possible; but there are those exhibitionists, the geese. It is easy to accuse them of avian braggadocio because they often fly so much higher than they need, even over the highest Himalayan obstacles. George Lowe, the climber, has observed a formation of bar-headed geese passing over the summit of Everest itself.

At this altitude the pressure is about a third that of sea-level. Oxygen is therefore reduced by a similar proportion. The temperature at 30,000 feet is lower by 90 °F than it is at sea-level but, as this is warmer than many birds frequently experience in Antarctica, or during the troughs of a nothern winter, it is air and energy that are the prime imponderables. Just how can the geese acquire sufficient oxygen to fly at those altitudes? Presumably they use thermals to achieve height, as birds so often do; but, even so, it is extraordinary that a physiological system able to work well at ground level can also function five and a half miles up at migration time each year. Men, as we know so well from the tales of mountaineers, can barely gasp their way to be almost level with the geese.

In fact, men suffer at much lower heights. Prolonged exposure above 20,000 feet will lead to all manner of bodily breakdown, with practically every organ that has been investigated giving cause for concern. Treatment is elementary: go downhill. Even at much lower heights, and on the contours where some people habitually live, there can be more insidious forms of malfunction. Fertility is one such problem, or rather infertility, there being less conception at higher altitudes for those who live there permanently, as in Peru. Such people have more corpuscles per unit of blood, a faster flow, larger right ventricles and other adaptations, but they do less well in general and are still at less than half the altitude of those migrating geese.

Altitude can also be used instead of migration. In a temperate climate a bird must arrange its breeding cycle so that the young are ready either to withstand the winter or to fly somewhere else. Birds in the Himalayas can be most dilatory about the date, some having eggs even in August, and also unconcerned about the nesting altitude. Snow partridges, snow pigeons and yellow-billed choughs have all been recorded as breeding at over 15,000 feet. Such facts should not imply that the Himalayan climate two or three miles above sea-level is gentle and placid; anyone watching our nightly efforts to invade sleeping-bags, when fully clothed and duvet-quilted within the feathers of whole flocks of birds, might imagine we had been caught out in Siberia during a cold snap in wintertime. As it was, the season was late April, it was a moderate year, the camp was in a sheltered spot, the breeze was tranquil, and we were already zipped within our double tents. If this was late spring, we muttered to ourselves, then what on earth was winter like?

Birds that breed high and late indicate that they have another way of escaping the onslaught of winter. They do not have to migrate, at least not in the normal globe-encircling sense of the term. They do not have to stick it out, like the puffed-out passerines of Europe longing for crumbs and coconuts. The Himalayan trick is simplicity itself: coast downhill as far as you wish to go. A thousand feet of altitude is, as had already been noted, equivalent to 280 miles of latitude. Therefore a glide of, say, 4,000 feet, a modest labour even for a fledgling, is equal to a straight flight south of 1,120 level miles. The one can be achieved in much less than a day; the other is a considerable endeavour.

There is another angle to this solution. During winter it is possible that more food is available higher up the slope. The snow may fail to cover a pine forest's floor or small streams at altitude may not freeze like slower-moving rivers further down. In both cases a bird can migrate uphill for food and then downhill for warmth again. There is no need to go great distances; merely up or down will do.

One famous inhabitant of this mountain world firmly merits special mention. It has close-linked relatives in North America and elsewhere, but in the Himalayas it has achieved renown. Noted climbers are among its promoters. Every Sherpa and porter has a tale to tell. Every walker in these hills will find himself looking, wondering and then questioning.

'Are these yeti tracks?' asked Toni Hagen, the authority on Nepal.

'Nobody else here, Sir,' replied his dark-faced, narrow-eyed companion.

I admit to considerable personal curiosity on this score. I stared at all snow-marks with more than normal zeal, but I must also confess to seeing nothing of any account. In the valleys lower down I would scan the other side, but I saw nothing beyond goats, the occasional so-called antelope and the very occasional man. I longed, I can assure you, to witness some shuffling, hairy, anthropoidal thing, momentarily reckless of its privacy; but I saw none. I pictured every aspect, the immediate photograph, the clear result, the confounding of experts, the cash and fame and clash of argument, but not—alas—the scene itself. However, the Nepalis were adamant. 'Of course it lives,' they said; 'there is no point in denying the fact.' I go along with them. Of course it lives. It will only die when there is no emptiness, no wilderness in which to hide its secret. Should the Himalayas be tamed, and should they be like the European Alps, strung about with wires of ski-lifts and cable-cars. the yeti will perish. Until then there is a place for it. Long may its tribe survive.

One day it did indeed look as if the yeti had struck. Out of the blue and over the porridge one of our Sherpas limped painfully into camp. He was whimpering softly and holding one hand with the other. Questions sprang to mind but had to be quelled while attention was paid to the wounds he disclosed. His right hand was lacerated, and the medical box, hauled uphill with such labour, came into its own. Ointments and bandages were applied and only afterwards did he reveal a far greater hurt around his shoulder. This prompted further queries but, once again, there were more urgent tasks. When the shoulder had been treated and when all was, if not well, at least covered up, he indicated yet more pain. This time there was embarrassment along with the suffering. Both his buttocks were as raw a piece of meat as I had seen for a long time and I was bursting with questions but, even more than before, medical duty had pride of place.

Eventually, securely embalmed within his bandaging, he hobbled off to lie down in a tent. The Sherpas now set about their normal business with tremendous zeal. They plainly knew some answers and were not for giving them. We looked about us. What enemy had attacked so savagely? What could possibly strike from a world so brilliantly lit with the morning sun? Nothing but snow, ice and rocks lay on every side; not one thing more. And why were those poor buttocks so fearfully damaged when his trousers, if not as new, were scarcely scathed?

Abruptly a new light dawned. Of course, of course. No wonder the embarrassment, first of the man and then of the men. There was ample cause for that largest wound of all. Later, and surreptitiously, each of us glanced at the place where the mishap must have occurred. There were the footprints, leading down the slope. There was the spot, near a lip of greater steepness, which he had chosen for himself on that bright and early day. And there were the marks where, with arms outstretched, body spread-eagled and bare-bottomed, he had slithered for several hundred feet until a flatter stretch had halted him. For anyone it would have been a most fearful punishment (and a lesson well learned about steep snow and ice), but for a Sherpa, with heroic legends to maintain, the affliction must have been intolerable.

It was also the day when we had to leave. Fortunately, a chilling breeze sprang up, making the departure from such a magnificent mountainous entanglement less galling. Unfortunately, as uphill walkers forget, the business of going down a slope is also exhausting in its jolting, skidding, toe-numbing way. However, we did make better time. Far too speedily we saw the last of the snow, the end of the dwarf rhododendrons and of those huge, wide-ranging views.

In one sense mountaineers have done a disservice to mountainous regions. By concentrating so much on the peaks they almost suggest that nothing worthy lies in between. This is nonsense. The peaks are such a minor part; the broad valleys are so colossal. There may be thirty or forty miles between one tall range and the next, with the bulk of those intervening miles being well below the regions of ice and rock so favoured by the mountaineers.

These valleys are rich with life, flowering, growing, singing. The ribs of snow and ice above them are sterile, or nearly so, and do not compare in the goods they have on show. There is grandeur high up, and savage beauty, and sufficient danger to challenge anyone; but, for me at least the valleys between have new kinds of wonder at every turn. The Himalayas are 3,000 miles by 1,000 miles of high ground, and they do contain all the highest peaks of the world, but far and away the larger part of this tremendous range is not sharp summits or even snow and ice. It is the vast and splendid valley land lying in between.

Down this and through this we walked. The garnets glistened brightly in the morning sun. The lammergeiers left their cliffs, gliding almost hesitantly at first as if debating in which country to feed that day. Thamangs passed by, the men reputed to have the purest Mongol blood of all. The chortens and other religious structures would enlarge in size as we descended. At times they would be spread along the path more frequently than mile-posts ever are. To walk around them keeping to the right is following custom and does not offend; but it is also wise. On that highway only those descending have much of a field of view; each person coming up will probably see no further than his toes. Such a man, borne down with half his own weight upon his back, is not able to leap sideways at the glimpse of approaching feet. He has the momentum and agility of any freight carrier elsewhere in the world.

Each evening there were fires again. Woodcocks would fly back and forth like fruit-bats in other areas. Occasional tsauris, cross-bred between yaks and cows, would snort by. The porters would sing again, a habit frozen into silence higher up. New warmth might be the only cause, or sudden libations of chang, an alcoholic soup of a beverage needing a spoon near the bottom of the bowl. Gradually, as we consumed their loads, used up fuel, and ate almost everything, the excess porters would be sent downhill, there being no need to pay them any more. Consequently, at each night's stop, there would be fewer and fewer of us around the fire. No longer were we the six and thirty-four, but just the six and the Sherpas and scarcely any more.

Wilderness

The steepest slopes had been most troublesome on the journey up and were the saddest on our return. They brought us speedily down from the heights. The rivers carving their way through each steep valley, became more and more conspicuous. Whether they will remain that way is less certain. Having the steepest gorges of any range, and being drenched each year with the floods of the monsoon, means that the Himalayas are richest of all in what is called white gold. Nowhere else is so suitable for hydroelectricity. These hills could become the great powerhouse of Asia, exporting energy north and south, entrapping over and over again the cleanest source of power, a bounty that returns in equal strength each and every year.

If that happens to any marked degree, yet another wilderness will surely start to lose its people. This, I had steadily learned, is the pattern of our day. However much we fill up the country areas, or think we do, it is a contradictory certainty that much of wilderness is being drained of life. There are no longer all the Eskimos there used to be. The Indians are yielding up Brazil. The Aborigines are choosing cheques to nothingness. The land they used to know was always bare but there is now a barrenness not there before.

In the Himalayan wilderness this is not so. There are as many people as ever there were. Occasionally there are husks of villages but these have been vacated not because new pressures have squeezed their ancient livelihood. Instead, old laws are still at work, with this or that place becoming a haunt of spirits or bad luck and not a place for men. It is eerie to pass through such a film-set of a settlement, stacked with houses, streets and stone-faced walls, and find it stripped of everyone; but the scene is only odd and never sad. The move is a local choice and not the tail effect of some economic shuffling half a hemisphere away. The real villages, still rich with occupants, are as they ever were. Their people turn out yet again to watch the passers-by and the visitors take another look at them. 'Do you watch birds?' someone asked of E. B. White. 'Yes,' he replied, 'and they watch me.'

Down further goes the path. Like an army in retreat we are now but a handful of our former numbers. We are also less of a bunch, with lethargy taking its toll, or chang, or an aftermath of the cold times earlier. There are different birds, like the black-headed shrike; there are more plants, like berberis; there are always more discoveries. Just how is it that the greenness of the pines makes the blueness of the sky so much more startling? Does no child in the area ever run out of maize? Their hands would delve into those coarse, patched jackets of theirs, seek out the pockets, burrow for maize, and always emerge with enough to chew on, and smile with, or spit with if need be.

At the last camp, a lawn of a place with the road in view, a flock of children accompanied us on the final ritual. Some of them were of an age to have a kukri in their belts. Others could barely walk but, nevertheless, wore the uniform of thick coat, thick cap and nothing below their knees. Those of us who had walked to the snows now strode with an easy arrogance. Muscles were finally in keeping with the task. Surplus fat had gone, and the lower altitude made every labour seem simple. All the same, the sight of the river was daunting. Admittedly, it had been our companion for some days, and we had watched it grow as it gathered strength along the way, but it looked more awesome as we stripped off our filthy clothes and prepared to join its turbulence.

To call it a bathe would be misleading. The grey-white waves thrashed round and over us, assuming more rocks were in their way. We groped for footing, found none, sought handholds in round granite, lunged at the soap, fell, slipped downstream a rock or two, stood and fell again, pinioned by water and capable only of seeing the gestures of delight from that patched and ragged row of children ranged along the shore. They laughed so much that they could neither spit nor chew. This was the scene they had come to see; it happened every time. These walkers from another world always finished up this way.

The alternative view was entirely different. Above that row of hats were the terraces set round the homes. Above them were more and more small green fields until either rocks or trees brought a change, a finality to all that labour. The trees lasted for a while and then, the altitude becoming too savage for them, they gave place to the grasslands. Eventually, as the crown, as the icing,

127

there were the white peaks, catching the sun from first to last. Only below them, where growth becomes possible, does life flourish. That was the feature of this wilderness. It had life. It had it not just abundantly but with extraordinary variety. In mere miles we had gone no distance, but in the range of our experience we had travelled from one end of the planet to the other. Let posterity know, and, knowing, be astonished, as they could phrase it two centuries ago, that in this instance and in this wilderness we had done it all by foot. Let posterity also have a chance of doing so.

6 *Tundra*

The Northwest Territories [of Canada] has everything to make it
the 20th century's most exciting place to be.
Commissioner of the NWT, Yellowknife

The visiting Martian, in reporting back to his planet about the
forms of nature here on Earth, would have mentioned those
excesses already encountered in this book. Having described ice,
forest, desert and mountain, he would then have turned his
attention to the final kind of wilderness, the last great empty
zone. It is the flattest, the wettest, and some say the most desolate.
It is the least known, the least likely to be beset with visitors. It
separates the true Arctic from the trees and is the most sharply
defined of all major biotic communities. There are millions of
square miles of it, virtually all in the northern hemisphere, and it
is called the tundra.

I do not know whether the Martian would hate cold or heat, or
find most joy in mountains or their opposite; but I know that I
had discovered immense beauty and wonder in every emptiness so
far. There had always been ample to compensate for the drawbacks
of climate; sufficient to occupy the mind whatever was inflicted
upon the body. I had been cold and hot, pinpricked by creatures
and plants; but had never regretted for a moment being in each
place. On the contrary I had felt overjoyed, happy, privileged, and

129

continuously amazed—but that was before I had met the part of this planet's surface that bears the name of tundra.

The books had not raised my hopes. 'The number of species that can endure the conditions is small ... Where drainage is better there is a dreary stretch of lichen and coarse grass with occasional hummocks of a brighter green where the home of an arctic fox or snowy owl enriches the soil with its refuse ... Sometimes a flower carpet brightens the otherwise monotonous landscape ... there is permafrost below the surface ... A walk is dampening to the feet, with 60 per cent of the land being shallow lake ... the cold can be more chilling than further north, and without the beauty afforded by snow and ice ... The mosquitos are more numerous than elsewhere ... There is no plant growth until mid-July ... September sees the start of winter.' It was possible to shiver solely on reading the literature.

I looked at the photographs. From the air it was a battlefield of lakes, like flooded shell-holes as far as the camera could see. From the ground there was always a straight horizon, wet land below, sky above. Captions were equally forthright: 'Water cannot drain away owing to frozen soil beneath and lack of slope in the land ... Plants that might be annuals elsewhere spread their growth— budding, flowering and seeding—over several years ... Few mammals can survive the cold. Most birds migrate south for the winter. There are no reptiles.' A stomach is never the most loyal of organs and mine contracted audibly.

Time, coupled with the experience of heading north from Winnipeg, north again from Churchill, and yet farther north as the ice relented, modified my views. Of course, the place would have virtues. Who could suggest that 9 per cent of the Earth's surface is devoid of them? There are deficiencies, certainly from the standpoint of a visitor spoiled by and drenched in splendours from other areas, but during my stay I encountered both good and bad. It was both supremely wonderful and extremely awful. I learned, in short, what is meant by a word more linked with textbooks than daily life. I learned about the tundra.

Take this day, for example, the day of the polar bear. The air was crisp, the sky cloudless. At sea there were still flecks of ice, but these were vanishing fast. On land there was great silence save on the promontory we had come to inspect. It was a rare sight in itself, a rocky protrusion jutting like an arrowhead from the shore; but on its southern side was an even rarer scene for almost all of us, a honking and a grunting and a stench of walruses. They looked superb. They sounded terrific and the smell immediately brought back happy memories of penguin rookeries. On board our boat we suddenly had to go ashore. There was no time to lose.

The canoe was lifted overboard. We clambered into it and its bottom was soon scrunching on the shingle of the shore. A final wave slapped at us and we fell on land much as the wave had done. We hurried up the slope, carrying our equipment away from more waves, and then remained at the dry points we each had reached. The air was welcoming and clean, with just a touch of walrus in it from the promontory's other side. It was great to be standing on new land once again.

Part of the surprise in suddenly seeing something is that it was apparently invisible beforehand. It was large enough and its white bulk by no means merged with the grey rocks on either side but we had entirely failed to observe it when heading for this stretch of shore. Once observed, the polar bear received particular attention. Not that it did anything; it stayed where it was, some eighty yards away. Not that we did anything; we were transfixed. A piece of the wilderness had come startlingly to life.

Two of our group were Eskimos and they hurried back to the main boat for, as they indicated, some guns. We three remaining watched the canoe depart, intensely aware of a dramatic shift in that day's circumstances. From the good fortune of finding walruses it had become easier, far easier, to think of the bad fortune that could arise should the bear stir from its indolence and come our way. Presumably the sun was still shining brightly, and the sky no less blue, but our attention was firmly focused on that solid shape not far away. Externally we were idle; internally we raged with energy. To run was foolhardy, as it might provoke an unequal chase. To swim was no less so, with such an aquatic beast for a rival. Even to slink away might break the spell, narrowing both the odds and the distance. Remaining stationary suggests little initiative, and somewhat dull as a policy, but mere action was the sole alternative.

Our ears told us of the canoe's progress out to sea, of the shouts to and from the bigger boat, of the outboard's gentle puckering and then its whine as the canoe, now presumably fully armed, was turned to head our way. It scrunched again on the shingle, and the previous quiet became the jaunty bravado of those who know that the balance of power has been suitably transformed. We laughed. We laughed a lot, until the high pitch of a giggle brought us back to earth.

The intent was to film as well as see those walruses. We had noticed the bear from the boat, but at that time it had been safely farther up the promontory from the groaning group of walruses. Hence our confusion at its unexpected change of place, and that brief taste of life as it used to be. Our flesh, for a while, had been meat. From planetary predator we had become temporary prey, a salutary experience. The day was now warm once more, the sky quite blue. There were flowers, stubby pincushions on the ground, and soon there came the noise of walruses. On the same wind was the full vigour of the smell, a fruitiness, an intensity that made us laugh again. We could not yet see the animals and I elected to approach them by a difficult route. This way, or so we thought, it might be possible for the camera to see both me and the beasts in reasonable proximity. (The price of being a performer had to be paid, in varying ways, over and over again.)

Anyway, I left the others and we clambered our separate routes. The silence fell once more and the stillness of the rocks became sullen in the sun. The day itself grew abruptly oppressive. I started to feel solitary rather than alone, and thought of fear again. The bear that had caused such a flurry of alarm was now out of sight, but increasing unease became my firm companion. I walked, scrambled and slowly approached the crowded source of all that sound and smell. In theory, therefore, I should soon have breasted the slope ahead of me. In practice, the accompanying dread increased quite steadily. Flesh became meat again. I shivered as I moved forward and felt extraordinarily afraid. I have never known a time so calm and threatening, and even the walrus gruntings could not dispel the quiet. So, for the second time that day, I stopped. My right foot was on a group of flowers. I saw that as I stood there, silently and with a pounding heart.

How easy it was scampering down the rocks! How simple to turn back! I saw the bear just where it had been, still white upon grey rock, and then I found the parting place where the others had gone with their whispered talk and their guns. When I caught them up they were on a bluff staring away from the walruses. They looked strange but stranger by far was their greeting. They were effulgent. They flowed over with rapture of a kind I had not noticed previously. I raised my eyebrows but they lifted their arms to indicate a rock not very far away. On it was another polar bear. A blood-red nose was buried deep in a carcase of meat. The sight was arresting, and so too the thought that at that spot I should have appeared had I continued on my way. They had assumed I had done so. They had also imagined, not unreasonably, that that meat was my meat. So I too stared at the ledge, tingled as never before, and waited for my heart to resume a normal pace.

The reference books and their relevant bear information had been helpful in their way: '*Thalarctos maritimus*, family *Ursidae*. Live mainly on pack-ice in polar regions of northern hemisphere. Most carnivorous of all bears but may also eat lichen or moss. Mainly eat seals, but also fish, sea-birds, stranded carcasses. Great wanderer, unlike most carnivores. Males even travel during winter but females make a den. Young, usually two, born late Nov. or early Dec. Very tiny at birth and need considerable care.' Such facts were useful but on that particular day I learned a few other points not mentioned in the books. I learned again about being afraid. I had met another predator, not quite face to face but near enough. I had walked once more within a wilderness.

Virtually all of the world's tundra is either in the Soviet Union or in Canada. These are the two biggest countries in the world and much of their territory is of the kind of land known as the barren ground. It is the wettest part of the Earth's surface; save, of course, for the oceans and the solid wetness of the ice-caps. In many tundra areas about 60 per cent of the land is covered with little lakes, never very deep, often extensive and counted by the million. The Canadian Arctic has been called the world's largest reservoir of fresh water, which it is, or quite the most inconvenient walking country for every non-amphibian, which it also is. The place is so wet that anyone sloshing through the coarse grass growing between the lakes will soon find himself sloshing through the short reeds actually in the lakes. He will become wetter, but the matter seems marginal at the time.

At all events, when hung about with drying clothes that evening, he will gasp with disbelief when a book tells him the place is a form of desert. The reason for such an assertion is the very low rainfall. The average precipitation of snow and rain combined is about eight inches a year, or much less than on many a desert around the world. However, true deserts are defined by the rainfall set against evaporation. In this context the tundra is not of their number because its rate of water loss is extremely small. The rainfall is modest but, with little evaporation to take it away, and scarcely any seepage through the permafrost, the water has no choice but to remain. The land is flat, honed smooth by the ice ages. Its water stays on its surface in many millions of little lakes and does so over millions of square miles.

At least, it does until winter comes. The lakes then freeze, starting with the shallowest. The land also freezes as its surface hardens like the underlying permafrost which never softens throughout the year. Walking is then a simpler business. There is no longer any confusion between the wet land and the wetter lakes. Everything is ice-hard; the open water, the land, the marshes in between. It is possible to travel in a straight line, insofar as there is desire to do so during wintertime. This is the dominant season. It starts early and is slow to yield its grip. Sea ice does not even melt in much of the Hudson Bay until the middle of July.

The long period of biological inactivity then ceases. Everything happens at once. The soil surface melts. The sun is there, visible and warming, for all (or nearly all) of the twenty-four hours. Plant growth starts. Insects multiply. The birds hatch out their young, having arrived in time to take advantage of the summer surge of life. Mammals, such as the hares, foxes and lemmings, eat energetically. The days are not hot (particularly for travellers who arrive via Delhi) but they are hotter than those so soon to come. At the place where we first stayed (near 64°N) the mean July temperature was 46°F. Such heat was maintained in August but during September it slumped to 33°F with that month's minimum being 8°F. Any plant or creature still imagining that the relative warmth of summer had come for good is swiftly disillusioned. Winter, with darkness and cold, is the mainstay of the year.

The plants have adapted to such a climate in various ways. In general, the seeding habit has been discarded in favour of vegetative reproduction. Aided by the sudden wealth of sunshine, they grow rapidly until they are nipped in the bud, or in flower or in fruit, when the chill of autumn puts an end to such behaviour. Oddly, in that swamp of a countryside, the plants can suffer from drought. Soil water may be as cold as ice, the soil itself acid with humus, and the dry wind and bright sun will demand considerable transpiration. Consequently, although the wet-footed visitor once again disputes a fact, many of the plants are xerophytes, having small leathery leaves well stocked with hairs to cover their stomata. It seems like conserving sand in a desert, but water does have to be preserved. So too energy. Tundra plants do not climb; neither do they possess spines or any sting or poison. A traveller from further south, say from the forests of Brazil, would be astonished at a vegetation that cannot attack in any way and all of which is edible.

However, he will feel at home with the insects. I thought I had learned a thing or two about mosquitos, particularly around the Bight of Benin (or Bite of Benin as some say) but I now know they only do moderately well in that heat of Africa. They are out-gunned and even outsized by their rivals 60° further north. In the tundra they can cover an arm so that more mosquito is visible than arm. They are distinctly larger and do not restrict their activities to night-time. Perhaps it is a forlorn wish to expect them to take food only during the brevity of an Arctic twilight; but it is disagreeable that they use every moment of the never-ending day. I bought much *Off!* from the Hudson Bay Company, suspecting it makes more profits than furs ever did; but I was bitten enormously. The stuff cannot be applied either continuously or on those personal parts that rarely but surely see the light of day. Never in Africa had I been bitten there. Whenever a breeze sprang up, whether freezing or just chilling, it was a joy because the mosquitos vanished and pleasure began again.

The tundra is more of a wilderness than anywhere else I had ever seen. It possesses everything that that word implies. It has unendingness, and barrenness, and a kind of nothingness. An ice-sheet is empty but without pretence to life. A desert is vast but usually possesses some distant lure, a line of hills, a mound, a clump of something green. The tundra just goes on and on. Firm walker that I am, I could lose all resolve in that eternity. Walking seemed a most senseless thing to do.

For example, there was the island where we had met the polar bear. It was our home for a number of days. I knew no people lived there, but there was one herd of caribou, several crowds of walrus around its edge, quite a lot of bird life on that same periphery, and presumably something more within its considerable interior. It was, after all, almost the size of England. So, one day, well wrapped against the cold of July, breathing steamily into the mist, hoping the drizzle would not bother to fall, I left the boat and set off inland.

The signs of the sea were soon left behind. So too the bones showing where Eskimos had been active in the past. I would glance back from time to time, remembering that a safe return was more likely to follow if I knew what the return journey should look like; but my thoughts were on the land ahead of me. It was flat, but that came now as no surprise and certainly made for simpler walking than in Nepal two weeks earlier. Contours were not a feature of this new place; nor, come to that, were streams. If the

---

There are 5 million square miles of tundra, the flattest and wettest region of the Earth save for the actual sea. Its flowers, as overleaf, often take three seasons to complete the annual cycle. Its mammals include polar bear, walrus—and incredibly hardy people, such as this Chukchi from Siberia or the Eskimos of Canada who, before modern man arrived, built these marker cairns.

ground is flat and waterlogged, I realised slowly, there will not be any rivers as there is no cause for them. However, as a kind of recompense, there were all the lakes, and past these and round these or straight through these I proceeded on my way.

The landscape did not vary greatly in its colouring. Admittedly the day itself was monochrome, with the mist settling as time wore on, but the rocks were grey and the grass was more grey-green than grasses ought to be. Nevertheless, I strode on, duvet-pink and orange-capped, a strident blob of colour invading all the land. Gradually, and out of the mist ahead, there came something else to see. I had walked miles, seen nothing of note, in fact nothing at all, and then there was this object almost straight ahead. It was white, and more like a post in shape than any other thing. It was stubby, like the final part of a snowman when all the other snow has gone, and was entirely on its own, apart from me. I made a direct course now, splashing, squelching, wading, and still it seemed to have no proper form. It was more upright than side-ways, and motionless—until it got up and flew away. It was my first snowy owl.

I walked on, placing stones on the tops of rocks to guide my eventual return. The mist was thicker and all sight of the coastline had long since gone. The land was wet, flat, cold and always pocked with lakes. The flowers, such as they were, grew best on the rockier parts. They possessed, in the main, what the books call dwarfed sub-aerial growth. Small wonder, one said to oneself on inspecting their cushion forms. With frozen soil and chilling dankness even at the peak of summertime they had every right to be as sub-aerial and dwarfed as plants could ever be.

Then, quite suddenly, and for the first time in this world wilderness tour, I could see no point in prolonging the walk. I was neither hungry, nor tired, nor lost, nor late, nor running out of light. I just saw no purpose in continuing. There was nothing in sight to attract, not a hint of difference. The walk had changed

---

Not until June does the Kolyma river of northern Siberia achieve its annual melt. There is no spring to speak of, but a brief summer before, in early September, winter grips once more.

from a moving curiosity, normally quite satisfying, into a stolid, steady plodding. I walked on but could not see the point.

I looked for fossils, and found none in that shield of ancient rock. I squeezed sphagnum moss, marvelling at Eskimo ingenuity. They dry it and use it as a kind of cotton wool, good for babies. I saw lichens, often growing taller than the plants. Just once I met a stream, the clearest I had ever seen, but it was no more than water running over rocks. It had no plants in it, no weed, no insects; nothing but its crystal clarity. On the far side was what Indians called muskeg, the springy vegetation that can sit upon a bog. I passed some shells where once the shore had been. I saw my owl again; at least, I presume it was the same. It flew off, vanishing more speedily this time. The mist seemed thicker, far thicker, and wetter, and soon it was running down my face. Flatness, coldness, monotony, sunlessness and now rain—I turned upon my heels, shivered, blew a drop from the end of my nose and made for home.

My filming companions were in the boat, crouching over a noisy pressure flame, when I returned. They said it was cold. I agreed. They said it was a very wretched place. I agreed again. They spoke, as soldiers often do, giving the impression that nowhere in the world can match home, with the pub on the corner, the right brand of beer, the perfect ambience. It is possible to be annoyed with such single-mindedness, a readiness to complain, a reluctance to see virtue; but, as I too hunched over that noisy flame, listening to lamentations and hearing of pubs 4,000 miles away, I sang that tune as well. It was miserable outside, bloody miserable. It was cold, dismal, dreary for mile after mile after mile. It was the 9 per cent of this planet's surface that, frozen for much more than half the year, is always distinctly cool and often foul. We had learned a thing or two about the tundra and were not liking what we had learned.

'Its vegetation has to contend with extremely adverse circumstances,' I read out loud from the open page before me.

'I'll drink to that,' said someone. 'Let's make a cup of tea.'

Our boat, the *Kanerk*, had been beached within a small inlet during our stay on the island. This was an empty place, with only us in view, but most suitable. Practically every explorer of the region must have beached his ship, or careened her, or anchored off such a spot as we had chosen. Frobisher, the first Englishman to spend much time in these latitudes, must have had a similar view when he landed intent on finding gold. Hudson was the first European to enter the bay named after him before he and others were set adrift by a mutinous crew. Had he reached a shore (and no sign of him was ever found), it would have looked as ours looked—stony, umpromising, and death as soon as winter came. The trappers and whalers who came afterwards, the traders, the prospectors—they would all have known our kind of shore. They too would have crunched over its shingle, been amazed perhaps at the extent of its tide, and noted the relative lack of shells and barnacles before setting about their business. We, for our part, made a cup of tea.

We also, for good measure, boiled a few eggs, fried caribou meat, found some bread, turned up the flame of paraffin and drank from a precious bottle before, those things completed, relaxing and thinking of sleep. The Eskimos on board were draped within the wheelhouse and the engine-room. We had a cabin to ourselves. At least, they called it that if only because, without wheel or engine, it had no other name; but a greater lack was space. We were a tall group, swollen fat with clothing, set about with boots and cameras, and we lay just where we found ourselves at the end of that splendid meal. It was not that the others were invading one's personal area; it would have been cramped with only one in residence. So we laughed, doused lights, and settled down for some hours of palsied wakefulness.

There was a porthole. I realised it had two bolts and a brass rim after, fitfully in sleep, nuzzling its shape. So I tried to tie myself in some more agreeable kind of knot. My companions, slumped like potato sacks, breathing like waste-pipes, were apparently at ease and I turned back to the porthole. It was, after all, a gateway to another world.

Outside everything was white with moonlight. The glass was none too good, making for haziness, but the bright whiteness would have shone through anything. There were stationary clouds above an extraordinarily stationary scene. Not a thing was moving; no creature of course, but no waves were either plopping on the shore or heaving out at sea. Everything was absolutely still. It was also entirely quiet. The hatch over our cabin coop was firmly in place. (The only other choice—of having it chillingly open—had been rejected.) As well as admitting no breath of air, it let in no sound, no hint of anything from the monochrome world outside. I felt as though I was in a bathyscaphe; seeing, but that was all. So I watched and watched; there was nothing else to do.

Had I expected anything to enter my field of view, which I did not, I would have imagined it first appearing at a distance. As it was, the bear appeared about six feet away. The black and white landscape was abruptly obscured by a great shape, as when someone stands in a cinema just ahead of you. I am sure I stopped breathing but I could hardly stop looking. What a sight! What an unbelievable beast! It snuffled over the ground. It sniffed at footprints, never staying long, moving slowly, and padding over everything with vast and shaggy feet. They turn in, the Eskimos had said, if the bear is fat but out when he is lean. These turned in almost to face each other. It was an enormous animal.

Fear started when it vanished from sight. Where had it gone? Could it climb on to our beached boat, making use of the single plank that took us to the shore? The Eskimos, with all their armoury, were a hold away. They were locked in their quarters, just as we were battened down in ours. Suddenly I heard a noise, the first to come from that silent scene. There was a crack, then a crunch, and then came quiet again. Something was being eaten. I worried, and then remembered the bone from which our steaks had been carved earlier that day. Of course, of course; but fear was still pounding helplessly. What if the bear, its appetite whetted with meat, should wish for more? Our prison-coop reeked of supper smells, for the plates and pans were lying on the floor. I stared through my solitary outlet to the other world, seeing still the same quiet sea, the whisps of cloud. Then, filling the frame, as cameramen say, I could abruptly see nothing else but bear. I swear it looked at me. I know I retreated a little from my vantage point, the animal being now no more than a foot away. Its nose was

140

smeared, presumably with blood. Its mouth was open a little and its breath hung in the air. Then, just as it had come, it vanished from my view. The scene was as it first had been; uncoloured, silent, and without a movement anywhere.

'Heh!' I said, in a loud belated whisper to the others.

'Huh?' they said, before going to sleep again.

In the morning we looked at the huge footprints wherever there was sand rather than shingle. The mist had lifted but the bear had vanished. Gradually the paw-marks also disappeared as the tide rose and crept towards our boat. Soon it would be time to go but, before leaving, the Eskimos wished to shoot some caribou. I went with them to see, as some say, the sport. We strode much as I had done the day before, ate up unconvincing miles, and then saw a group of six against the straight horizon. If I was expecting also to see low cunning I was to be disappointed. With the others, I walked towards the group, lingering a few feet behind them, and stopped the moment they did. Those with guns lay down on the ground, took aim, fired, and fired again. As a result five of the caribou lay down in their turn. I immediately believed in a small tale I had been told. 'Where', said a visitor to an Eskimo, 'do you aim for with caribou? An inch ahead of the ear perhaps?' 'No, we just shoot and shoot until enough of them are dead.'

Enough had fallen down for us. We inspected their bodies and looked at the sixth animal, still in the area and half longing to be part of our company. It would walk to within fifty yards and then, impulses working erratically, wander quickly off again. Its pelt looked like scraggy underfelt. Its antlers were also furry at that time of year and bleeding from mosquito bites. There was not another caribou in sight; in fact there was nothing as far as the eye could see. The surviving beast would have been shot too but for the size of the heap upon the ground; we already had more than sufficient. Someone went to bring the canoe nearer and, after removing the intestines and quartering the carcases, we lumbered towards the shore with our bloody load. A few ring-plovers got up as we reached the pebbles of the beach. Then some terns chattered as we thumped our loads upon the ground. One bird, presumably with young not far away, first hovered and then attacked. Having dived, it then hovered again, waiting to swoop once more. An Eskimo, the broadest of the bunch, slowly scooped a pile of shingle with his hand, hesitated, and then threw it at the tern as it next dived down at him. I looked at the meat, and at the man, and at the bird, still surprisingly alive. Luckily there was work to do and I flung the flesh into the canoe with savage energy.

A few days later we were back in harbour again. With the boat we had seen a great deal, and we had seen the tundra where it is most active. The shoreline is relatively crowded with living things but one small island, looking smooth as we approached, seemed quite devoid of life, notwithstanding the Eskimo shouts. Suddenly the entire carapace of that piece of rock seemed to heave itself up, fragment, and slide heavily and noisily into the sea. All about us then were walruses, transforming the water's clarity into brown soup wherever they moved. A group surfaced very close to us, breathed indignantly and stared with pink and bloodshot eyes. A lone walrus at New York's zoo had caused no end of money, drugs and local expertise to be spent because it too had stared that way. Finally, and despairingly, a cable had been despatched northwards to a certain Eskimo. His reply was brief: 'WORRY WHEN WALRUS EYES LOSE PINK COLOURING UNTIL THEN OK.'

We also saw guillemots. By a cliff many thousands were in the air, either high or skimming in skeins just by the water-line. Someone fired a gun. It was like striking a wasps' nest or hitting a hive. Where there had been thousands there were suddenly tens of thousands if not hundreds of thousands. 'So much the better,' replied Leonidas, when a messenger had told him Persian arrows would darken the sky. 'We will then be fighting in the shade.' Our sun too was eclipsed by the numbers of birds that day. On the seaward side we saw white whales, the belugas making a come-back from their devastation a century ago. A few had young with them, offspring born weighing 1,300 lb., and all were idling by the edge of a great sheet of ice. This was the remnant of a compressed and jagged piece of pack, melting fast but still stretching for miles; quite a sight for the last week of July.

Our base was on another island to that of the walruses. It totalled 30,000 square miles and possessed one community of about 200, almost all of whom were Eskimos and most of whom were children. Before European man landed on these north Canadian shores (surprisingly early, considering their climate and the warmer pickings further south) there were 22,500 Eskimos. The figure is precise, suspiciously so, but it appears in many books and so appears in mine. Apparently, there were Eskimos as soon as the retreating ice permitted people to take advantage of the new and open land. About 6,000 years ago, in a migration quite distinct from that of the American Indian, the Eskimo ancestors moved into Alaska from Siberia and then proceeded eastwards. These people settled throughout the north Canadian tundra but then, roughly 1,000 years ago, became extinct. A further wave set out from Alaska, emboldened by a gentler climate, and it too spread over the area. Its people were well established when European man, frozen, rachitic but remorselessly adventurous, sailed first to that cold new world. Martin Frobisher, already noted for his optimism in gold, was no less straightforward over his first Eskimo. The ship's crew called him the Man of Cathay, felt delighted at having so plainly discovered the gateway to China at a stroke, and showed him off on their return to England (where he swiftly died).

Unlike genocidal activities elsewhere, the worst being Tasmania where every former inhabitant died within a century of European settlement, no one wished to destroy the Eskimo. Nevertheless, to a considerable extent, that is what happened. All isolated groups are vulnerable to infection from more crowded societies where diseases are most able to flourish, but isolated groups in cold climates are even more susceptible. Epidemics raged and Eskimos died. The explorers sometimes bartered guns or food for their services and, once again, Eskimos often died. In time these indigenous people, formerly so self-reliant, came to depend upon the foreigners and, if trade shifted elsewhere or a market fell apart, that dependence was disastrous. Once again the local people died. They had withstood fearful living conditions and the most inhospitable landscape, but they could not compete with the onslaught from the Western world.

Today everything is very different. The base where we stayed,

and to which the *Kanerk* returned, told us next to nothing of the
old days but much about the present. Its 200 people all lived
within flat-roofed, rectangular dwellings perched a couple of feet
above the ground. The area was strung about with wires, for
electricity, for the telephone, for washing. At ground level, as is
becoming a refrain for these wilderness communities, there was
much debris from the past—packing-cases, machinery, old
refrigerators (no difficulty in selling these to Eskimos) and cans
and bins and drums galore. The predominant noise came from
Japan via the balloon-tyred, two-stroke, three-wheeled, runabout
Honda scooters that everyone seemed to own and use, adult
pedestrians being a rarity. There were children in abundance and
families were large. Even in that modest hamlet two of the
mothers had ten kids apiece. There was a hospital, a church, a
Hudson Bay Co. shop, a co-operative store, a school, a garage, one
two-roomed hotel and a wharf.

We landed on that wharf and were repairing to the hotel on our
return. It happened to be 4 a.m. and one young man who came to
watch fell into the water during our disembarkation. As its
temperature was not much warmer than 30°F there was an
immediate flurry of activity to get him out again. He had stolen
drink, he said, from a Canadian official. His problem, therefore,
was alcohol, despite the community's voluntary ban on the stuff;
but a secondary reason for his loss of balance had been a pool of
blood still oozing from a dead dog. At the community's monthly
meeting the evening before there had been three major recom-
mendations. The first was to continue the restrictions on the sale
of drink. The second was to give good wishes to the official whose
marriage was imminent (and for whom the drink had been
imported) while the final item had concerned the stray dog
problem. It was decreed, and subsequently put into effect, that
every animal not housed within a home would be summarily shot
at midnight or thereabouts. As we disembarked, helped the young
man (transformed from happy drunk into very frightened
individual) and then picked our way to the Ell Hotel past canine
corpses, we were plainly losing no time in coming up to date with
recent happenings.

I kept on seeing the Canadian Arctic, despite gross dissimi-
larities, in terms of the Australian desert. Few fly almost directly
from one to the other, and therefore I cannot compare notes with
other travellers, but there were great parallels. Neither the dry
land nor the wet tundra was welcoming for settlement. Those who
had succeeded in these places had had their way of life turned
upside-down, however unintentionally. The relevant govern-
ments, whatever their motives, were attempting to heal injustice
with money, by supplying basic needs and weekly cheques. In
both places there is a sort of wish from authority that the old life
should continue, and certainly the Eskimos were able to hunt in a
way no ordinary Canadian can do. The Aborigines dump cars. The
Eskimos abandon their skidoos with similar laxity, leaving them
on the snow wherever they fail, either to sit on land when the snow
has gone or vanish within the Hudson Bay. (Over 700,000 of these
monstrous machines are sold annually in Canada. The Eskimos, I
swear, take greatly more than their share.)

Both the native Australians and their Arctic counterparts caused
me to ponder on a statement frequently put about these days. In
various ways it says that primitive men were in harmony with
nature. It suggests that such men were so strongly in unison with
the natural world that their lives did not offend the prevailing
balance. They killed when need be, as the lion kills. They did not
slaughter like a fox in a chicken-run. They took only what they
wanted, were few in number, had occasional ritual wars with their
fellows and never murdered their environment as modern man has
done. I believe this picture to be a false one. I think that early man
was as frightening, thoughtless and damaging as his modern
successors, but merely lacked the means to fulfil these later
tendencies. Today's Eskimo, thumbing through the
mail-order catalogue for more exciting purchases, is certainly
unlike his struggling ancestor but he made me doubt, time
and again, whether his forefathers actually did lead a life of
harmony.

I found it easier to believe that early man, rushing through the
new world of America, was responsible for the extinction of the
many mammal species which perished at that time. I have never

seen a hint of any act among primitive communities that I could label as conservational. Conversely, there has often been a squandering of resources, such as overkill, or leaving poison in a stream when the fishing is done, or a wantonness of destruction that seems to serve no point. To my mind, harmony with nature did not exist; swat a mosquito, throw rocks at a tern, fish for the sake of it, kill to excess, shoot (or spear) a walrus to feed a dog, take according to inclination, grab, hunt, trap, and let the morrow take care of itself. Numbers were small, and therefore the damage was less than it might have been; but, to let this argument run its course, I believe the populations were modest partly for the very reason that conservation was not a feature of that ancient style of life. There was no husbanding of resources, no killing of males in polygamous communities rather than females, no taking only according to need, no thought of safeguarding stocks. This is all belief as, *faute de mieux*, it has to be; but, before my journey, I too had thought in terms of harmony. I no longer did.

Our settlement was an odd place to live. As in many of the world's colder places, the heat inside our home (and everyone else's) was intense. An oil-fired metal stove apparently (and reasonably, at times, no doubt) had no gauge-setting lower than maximum. The telephone was equally forthright and rang repeatedly. Everyone talked at length. Dial a wrong number and a great quantity of Inuit would assault your ears, English being a rare ability. Dial for the operator and Ottawa would answer from 1,500 miles away. In fact, as the call would first have to leap from our village's huge saucer-shaped transmitter to a satellite before bouncing down to the Canadian capital, the distance involved was nearer 50,000 miles; but the answer was always immediate. Its very swiftness and clarity emphasised rather than diminished our isolation. Over that glowing heater, through the window, past a posse of parked three-wheelers, beyond the dead dogs, above the wharf so twisted and crushed by each year's ice, and way out far, far beyond the cleanly-etched horizon, there was this girl with her headphones; courteous, warm and wildly inaccessible. Even the nearest village was 200 miles away. From most points of the compass there was no human of any kind for many more hundreds

146

of miles, let alone a girl, velvet-voiced, soft in her chuckles, who could be summoned, genie-like, just by dialling 0.

There was a road leading from our village. It travelled for ten miles and then expired on meeting the runway. Almost all the tundra communities were without a connecting road and even Churchill, much further south and a major port on the edge of the tree-line, had no road between it and the rest of Canada. Our track was outstandingly busy and had accidents, bizarre events for such a little place; but, if you owned a powered bike (and who did not?) the road was waiting from the moment a packing-case had been forced to yield its contents. Walking in the village was difficult as three-wheeled things skidded past among the rocks, houses, children, each other and you. On the road life was even less secure. Hunched figures, wrapped in furry parkas, accompanied by a high-pitched noise from 8,000 revs., would hurtle past as if with urgency only to hurtle back before silence or dust had settled down again. 'There must be some other way,' we said, having experienced the road, having failed to ride those bikes across the landscape, and having walked laboriously to no great distance or effect. 'There must be a better way of getting about in this tundra countryside.'

Then we found the Bombardier. Within moments of its discovery, and having handed over a weight of cash (something has to pay for those mail-orderings), we were joyfully in the middle of a most awful vehicle. It was as loud as a tank. It had a tank-like field of view, the windows being modest things. It even had rotating tracks with which to grip the ground plus two front wheels that touched it casually and made brief stabs at steering as we lumbered on our way. Despite similarities it was not a tank; it was a Bombardier. Worth every penny, it lurched and slewed and roared towards regions that we had never seen before. It too was confused between sodden land and reedy lake; but we, amidships, would know the depth of water simply by looking at the floor. In lakes it poured in through the doors; on land it gurgled out again. Mosquitos would fly in, heaven knows how, but would swiftly perish from the heat, the noise or, for all I know, the depths of swift despair. Beneath us the tracks would grip, fling aside a spray

147

of mud and crawl up and over rocks with no hurt to the machine save at those spots where our heads collided with its steel.

After an hour we came to the edge of a cliff. We waded to the door, jumped out into a lake, discovered that our hearing remained partially intact and were absolutely enchanted with the view. It is worth reiterating that good tundra views are thin on the 5 million square miles of tundra ground. What we were seeing then was not another expanse of flat, wet bog; it was a wondrous view. At the foot of the cliff was a broad river, spilling over rocks, and snaking through its walls on either side. Upstream, it vanished where a final bend took it from our sight. Downstream, it flattened out, eased its pace as the journey neared its end and imperceptibly changed its rhythm into that of the sea. It looked as a river should look, and as a million rivers do look. There was no novelty in the sight, save that we had not seen its like for many lake-filled, bog-filled, horizontal days. It was, we said to each other more than once, emphatically a view.

With cliffs a rarity, any such steepness was certain to be occupied. As our ears regained their powers we heard the call of a hovering, swooping, soaring peregrine. With the clarity of a mine-detector, while we climbed and walked along the cliff the bird chattered all the louder as we drew nearer to its nest. I remembered childhood days with binoculars and new boots, searching among Welsh hills for a glimpse of this same species; but here, suddenly and only several feet away, was a nest containing three balls of fresh-hatched falcon fluff. The parent bird seemed to relax once we had found its ledge, and circled silently. We looked at the nestlings, at their cliff and the stream beyond; it was indeed a very splendid view.

Besides, there were more flowers. Better drainage and the rockery of cliffs meant many species were flourishing quite abundantly. There were saxifrages and buttercups, oleanders and bilberries, sandworts and louseworts. There were even, in a few rare spots, some willows and alders, growing more as a thicket than as trees. There were still mosquitos, and any inadvertent backward step more probably encountered bog than rock, but there were a lot of flowers. The horizon was as straight as ever, direct propaganda for flat earth societies; but the wide stream, its union with the sea, the plants, the cliffs and the hovering peregrine made it all quite different. We had lunch there. We idled about and even kicked the Bombardier affectionately for having brought us to that spot.

'Wouldn't mind living here,' someone actually said.

In the context of the tundra, and in the wake of statements made on other days, it was a staggering remark.

It was also perceptive. During our wandering we stumbled across some stone circles. Nearer the sea the area was extremely rocky, having more stone than turf; but, as we leapt from rock to rock, we suddenly realised that some had plainly been arranged. Huge boulders formed near-perfect circles, save where single gaps led either to the outside or to an inner circle similarly made. People had lived here. In the old days (and no one could say when) these had been Eskimo houses. Over and above these round bases they had made a roof, arched with whale ribs, covered first with skin and then with earth or moss. Such dwellings were their homes for the bulk of every year. Everyone else knows that Eskimos live in igloos, but Eskimos assert that they only built the blister-like snow houses during hunting trips in wintertime. In summer they would often erect temporary shelters, again with skins and bones, to cut down on mosquitos by catching the breeze. But for the bulk of their lives, particularly the women and children, home was the kind of place that we had found and on whose stones we stood.

All around, now we came to look for them, were teeth, skulls, limb-bones, sharpened fragments, bits and pieces from the past. That river must have provided good char. There would have been many caribou. At sea, or resting on the shore, there were certainly seals and walruses. Occasionally, creating a bonanza to beat all others, the men would have killed a whale, an art that only the second wave of Eskimos had mastered properly. This way of life had times of plenty but also, no doubt of that, desperate times of lack. Children were placed under the ice; so too the useless old. Today's Inuit (the proper name for Eskimos) claim that wars form no part of their history, a laudable record; but, with one person for each 250 square Arctic miles, the pressures were never of overcrowding. That density equals 200 people in all England living as a single community near, say, Felixstowe. Their nearest neighbours would be 120 others living, perhaps, by Inverness: a long trip for a visit of any kind.

We stood on the stones and thought of the most awesome danger ever to come that way. Someone would have shouted on seeing the tall sails. Everyone would have rushed to the beach. Eventually, when the enormous ship had anchored off the headland, the men would have launched the whale-boats and initiated the contact that was to put an end to their ancient ways. The stone-age community saw iron and wood and longed for it. They saw guns and wanted them. By bartering fresh meat they got such things, along with disease, dependence and ultimate despair. Their numbers fell. They abandoned old homes, such as the one beneath our feet, took jobs, lived aboard the whalers, moved into settlements, met missionaries (who invented a script for them), accepted welfare, inoculations, schooling and money, before finally recovering something of their former strength. Their population increased (it will soon be similar to the old days) and much of their pride returned. The past had gone but the new days are not bad. 'Draw me an Eskimo scene,' a teacher once said to a well mixed group. The whites all drew igloos, kayaks, snow. The Eskimos, no less decidedly, drew houses, skidoos and aeroplanes.

Up above those rings of ancient homes we found their graves. With digging impossible, because of rock and solid permafrost, burial was a surface business. The bodies would be laid on the ground and then covered with rocks. These might not keep off the bears but would at least prevent foxes from gnawing at the meat. Farther up the hillside than those long and poignant mounds were two tall pinnacles of stone. Unlike European cairns that crown mountains with molehills made of rock, these were elegant and slim. They stood sentinel as guide-posts, but now they guide no more. Below them were the graves, then the circles, the cliffs, the river and the sea. The falcon still flew silently near its nest. In the good times, it must have been a pleasant place to live, at least for the tough, resourceful, resilient, independent Inuit.

One person to each 250 square miles, eight inches of rain or snow annually, darkness for more than half the time, freezing temperatures for three-quarters of the year, plant growth for six weeks or so, ice on the sea for most months, animals either present in fair numbers or suddenly absent, all food acutely seasonal, few raw materials, biting flies in summertime, biting cold in winter—the bare Arctic tundra facts are bleak. However, people did survive in this huge and empty buffer zone separating the permanent ice from the warmer lands with trees. They still live there, buttressed by money and help from further south; but, with deep-freezers outside every doorway, that vast satellite dish for instant talk, powered skis for winter and wheels for summertime, the kind of life has changed beyond all measure.

What has not changed, and will not, is the world beyond those overheated doors. It will always be flat, cold, wet, and the 'land of a million lakes' as the brochures call the area. It has now been cleared, for the main part, of its enormous herds of caribou. The whales, seals and walruses are not as they used to be. The people, seduced as elsewhere into settlements, are no longer so scattered, no longer such people of the wilderness. Since the ice retreated almost a tenth of this planet's land has been tundra land. This wilderness, like the ice, like the deserts, will not swiftly disappear. The more I saw of its daunting qualities the more assured I felt of that. For one thing, I was almost glad when the moment came to go.

7 Swamp

I would think twice of an Englishman's view of his neighbour but would trust implicitly his account of the Upper reaches of the Nile.
Washington Irving, an American.
The Upper Nile has no ancient histories to charm the present with memories of the past; all is wild and brutal, hard and unfeeling.
Samuel Baker, an Englishman.

In point of fact it was quite difficult to leave our Eskimo village. A fog settled over Churchill, several hundred miles to the south, for the best part of a week. Aircraft to it and from it were stranded up and down the Northwest Territories, schedules awry, routes disoriented. People clogged hotels, occupying rooms and telephones, obsessed with commitments in other areas. It was a stalemate, a confusion between the natural world and the man-

---

Swamps are the most threatened wilderness areas on Earth. Mankind longs to drain them and frequently does so. But people such as Dinkas, animals like the Mississippi alligator, and pitchers and scores of other plants need swamps if they are to live in the wet world that is their special form of home.

152

made hurly-burly of moving bodies from place to place. 'Curse this fog,' people would say, blaming the one innocent factor in the whole dotty chain of events.

What with abortive excursions to the airstrip based on false rumours, retreats to the hotel and the continued presence of the brooding Churchill fog, it was a period lavish with bits and pieces of extra time. Wanderings away from base had to be short, in case a plane should suddenly arrive. So I would walk through the village, dodge the traffic, admire the good sense of locating deep-freeze units out of doors, push kids on swings, try to write my name in Inuit, fail to admire the bone and soapstone carvings that were on sale, observe the corpses (of dogs or seals or walruses) and end up by the rocks of the local cemetery, the final outpost of every Arctic settlement. There were still mounds of stone as in the old days; but, within them, instead of bodies lying naked, there were coffins made of deal. The letters on these former packing cases were clearly visible: This Way Up, No Hooks. At one end of each grave, and fixed through the rocks, would be a cross, equally simple in its carpentry. Generally it had no words or, at most, a single name, the barest reminder, the briefest epitaph. To one side of each cemetery was the village, spread beneath its cat's-cradle of wires and laundry lines. On the other side, on every other side, there was the tundra, so full of lakes, so steeped in wilderness.

Inevitably, with time to spare, my notebook was to receive further jottings as thoughts came to mind. Once again, here are a few.

How odd to see an animal actually wild. Effort is necessary to realise it was not placed there by human agency.

A zoo permits familiarity with, say, a polar bear, but destroys none of the excitement in seeing its wild counterpart.

The Danube river meets eight countries in an orderly manner before, still reluctant to reach the sea, it spreads out into a magnificent delta that is one of the world's great swamps.

Wilderness

Walking in the wilderness is making your own path and having little idea what will happen, a deliberate intrusion but without any other goal.

Wildernesses should be contemplated at their most extreme, as the tundra in wintertime, with darkness, cold and nothing to do.

It is quite different going along any path a second time. So many variables have changed.

Commercially the world's wildernesses are parasitic; so too their people. But what a miserable criterion this can be.

Lie down to rest and a skua will come from nowhere to look at you. All virtues are then no more than the potential food encased in a body.

How can imagination hope to grasp even the barest idea of some past event. The ice to smooth this rock was probably one mile high. What an impossible notion!

There is every form in nature but a straight line. To see even an approximation of one, such as the sudden start to a fog-bank, is startling.

Why is there such enthusiasm for killing? For some, of course, it is a way of life. But even city people will shoot, for sport, for the pot, for nonsensical conservational reasons, for alleged defence. There is alacrity to kill, however flimsy the excuse, and no detectable remorse after doing so.

Why are primitive people so susceptible to alcohol and other drugs?

The Eskimos longed to see Antarctica. What joy it would be to take a group down south.

The wilderness I walk through does not so much belong to me as to no one. Therefore I feel an immediate personal involvement not permitted elsewhere.

People sue a US national park if an animal attacks them. No such thought could possibly come to mind in a wilderness.

I never saw anyone else walking, save for a very definite purpose. Can it be solely a modern habit?

People who live in the empty parts of crowded countries often say they are in the wilderness, being ten miles or so from the nearest store. A true wilderness is of a totally different magnitude.

Such utterances, as I had called them earlier, were scarcely conclusive, but by worrying and gnawing at different aspects of all the various areas, I began to acquire a composite appreciation of their

154

attributes. In one sense they were all the same place: the desert was a forest and an ice-cap and a mountain. It became increasingly possible to see wilderness as a single entity, whatever its furnishings. I began to observe what they supply that other areas lack. It is not just space, or clearer air. It is the absence of control, a different set of rules, a world within our world, to which it should not be compared. 'Give me again O nature your primal sanities,' said Walt Whitman, getting to this point. Out in the wilderness there were new longings, new lusts. In the presence of nature 'I am glad to the brink of fear,' said Emerson. I like that even better. In many a wilderness such gladness was a fearful part of it. There was a catching of the breath, over and over again. Just one flower could do it, or a view, or a single polar bear.

There was still one form of wilderness that I wished to see. Like tundra or desert it could deny forms of life; but, unlike those two and other barren areas, it had always been vulnerable to mankind's tinkering. It was widespread in the past, far more so than now, but its destruction could always be achieved fairly readily. Quite simple technologies would do the trick, and frequently did so because water running over land is so susceptible to change. Untamed swamps were, therefore, the final form of wilderness that I wished to see.

Paul Brooks, the American conservationist, once wrote: 'As any small boy knows, the presence of running water is a compelling reason to build a dam. Most boys when they grow up turn to other things, but a select few go on to join the US Army Corps of Engineers.' The remark is unfair and true. We have all seen dams, sluices, straightened waterways, canals that once were streams, and we have seen the kind of engineering which turns a lake into a reservoir. Water, if left to itself, is so disorderly. It obeys gravity, but in a slipshod manner, wandering this way and that, changing its pace, eating at its banks, even altering its route from year to year. Worst of all, if the slope is unduly gentle, the water can lose heart, forget its former purpose in heading for the sea and spread itself indulgently on the flatness of the land. A twisting river, making its own rules, is a kind of awfulness for the engineer. A bog of any kind is infinitely worse. Morass, marsh, slough, sump, quagmire—even the words have a cloying ring to them. To the conscientious engineer, the existence of unchannelled water is a challenge, and the sight of any bog is hard to bear.

One can see his point. A bog wastes water, directly by evaporation, indirectly through all the leaves that it supports. It wastes land. It is unfit for navigation. It is vague in its outline, oscillating with the seasons and quite undisciplined. Besides, the ailment can be cured so simply, creating blessings of a kind all along the line. One straight ditch through the middle, made only a little deeper than the bog itself, will soon have all the water running through it. The land will dry up, yielding huge new pastures. River traffic will begin and water loss will be reduced. Lock gates, weirs, dams, spillways and all manner of other contrivances will produce much gain. A river will have been brought to heel.

This was the pattern of events long before anyone could work with concrete or think of turbo-generators. Even the simplest tools, as children know, can help to make a stream out of a morass. Time and again bogs must have paid the price of their vulnerability. There was no need to finish the job at once. A little channel here, some extra drainage there, and each such effort would have been rewarded by more land to plough, easier access, better fishing and a more controlled environment. Much of the flat agricultural portion of the world must have been bog in days gone by, but those days have long since gone. The bogs were, in their way, another wilderness. They were inhospitable to men. They made difficult walking country. They could even kill if the soil was suitably glutinous. They did not have to be enormous; even the smaller ones could stop development and that, in the main, is what permits a wilderness. It was therefore one more kind of land upon my list.

I thought it fitting that it should be the last. The other sorts of wilderness were not immutable—there will surely be less forest in the years to come, less desert if water is suitably arranged—but there is an urgency about the swamps that makes their case more pressing. I had been, for example, to the Danube's delta, seen its problems, watched its tourists, observed the local industries of fish and reed, and marvelled at all the birds making energetic use of the river's complicated ending before it met the sea. Conflicting pressures there are colossal. What is good for boats is bad for almost anything else. What is good for men is almost always wrong for birds. A swamp of any kind, whether it is a delta or simple morass, possesses more immediate conflicts than any other sort of wilderness. It is an apt conclusion to a tour round the world.

But where? There are bits and pieces of bogs in many areas. I spun the globe once more, and looked up specific spots, but it was a memory from the past in Africa that seemed suddenly most germane. I remembered that occasion primarily for its extra-ordinary journey. Never before, or since, have I spent such a continuous length of time on board a boat; yet the voyage was on no ocean but firmly within a continent. Every morning I would climb the mast, search as a mariner might do for signs of land and see nothing but papyrus on every side. For day after day, while the boat's paddle-wheels thumped us to the north, there was that same old view. I would descend to the deck, eat three times, sleep and climb at dawn to see yet again that eternity of waving fronds stretching to the horizon everywhere. It was an amazing, unforgettable experience. The place was called the Sudd. It was also, which I could well believe, the largest inland swamp the modern world had ever known. So, of course, I now longed to see it again.

However, during my globe spinning, I had come across a lesser swamp within the American state of Georgia. It had the pleasing title of Okefenokee and, although it must be wrong to be guided by a name, this did exert appeal. So too the fact that it possessed alligators, ospreys, tall stands of cypress and was said to be the best managed swamp in all America. It too had pressures—timbermen, drainage experts, highway enthusiasts, scientists, seekers after turpentine—but it still existed. So how could I add it to my list? The simplest of solutions suddenly came to mind.

'Let's visit both swamps,' I said. 'Let's see the biggest swamp there has ever been, and then let's see how such a place can possibly survive; the one will complement the other.' I should thereby finish my globe-encircling year with a flourish; visit the Sudan, linger there, and then move from the old world to the new. Second, then, to Okefenokee; but, first, once more, into that Sudd.

The word means blockage. Roman legions were unaccustomed to withdrawal, but Nero's soldiers failed to make a passage through this barrier. The White Nile was a highway into the dark continent, and the Sudd sat impenetrably across this river. Modern machines have battered a single twisting channel through this ancient obstacle; but, apart from this one tenuous waterway, the rest of the Sudd is as it ever was. It had stopped the ancient Egyptians. It had halted the Romans and every other expedition until steam power arrived in the nineteenth century. How could a mere swamp be such a fearful barrier? Surely I should at least try where the others had failed?

Orde Wingate said no jungle should be considered impenetrable until it had been penetrated. He would have been proud of his disciple. I bicycled to the edge of the swamp, leaned my machine against a stand of reeds and prepared to invade. The Sudd's beginning was most precise and at once I stepped inside. The first yard was pleasant enough, with gentle fronds keeping the sun at bay. I am less certain about the second yard because I slipped and, in slipping, aroused a swarm of mosquitos, doubtless amazed at good fortune come their way. The third yard was plain sailing. Having stood on an angled papyrus stem I fell most swiftly to land upon my back. All progress so far had occurred more or less at ground level, but the fourth yard was different. After standing up, determined to tread on no more stems, I strode purposefully forward and disappeared inside a pool. Even the mosquitos were taken by surprise for they now flew, lit by shafts of sunlight, where I had been a second earlier. It was a deep pool but became shallower as I clawed up its banks until I stood again roughly at the height that I had been. My mosquitos, refusing to become embroiled lower down, were waiting for me to rejoin them before they pounced once more. Five yards done; 200 miles to go. I began to understand what made a legionary turn back.

The Sudd sits on 14,000 square miles of land. At the time of the annual flood, when water from the rains down south has reached the area, this size is doubled, making the swamp half as big as

England, almost as big as Maine. It is, of course, quite flat and the major plant to sit on it is *Cyperus papyrus*. This single species provides 97 per cent of the Sudd's biomass, a kind of dominance probably unequalled in any other place. The plant is most vigorous, growing at four inches a day, which in terms of bulk creates another record. Just by spreading from some central point it can cover an extra quarter of a mile every single year. Such energy requires a lot of water to keep it going. The total annual flow of the Nile passing through Juba on its way to meet the swamp is 27 thousand million cubic metres. The total flow at Malakal on the swamp's other side is 14 thousand million cubic metres, a 48 per cent loss to the atmosphere. This is equal to two and a half times the volume of water used in England and Wales during the same period. The world's largest swamp therefore has giant facts to match its size.

After my brief foray, which transformed a pink-shirted individual into, so they told me, a mottled salamander, I crawled out, largely upside-down, the bog still bubbling in my wake, mosquitos drinking to the last, and thought only of the swamp's splendid name. Sudd is 'blockage or barrier' according to the dictionary. 'How very apt,' I thought, pulling mud from my hair, hoping to observe a lost gym-shoe and seeing only the feeble indent I had made. 'Sudd,' I added; 'it even sounds just right.'

The Romans, one assumes, must have thought of going round the obstacle. Perhaps they did (history does not relate) but this would not have removed the barrier. It would have meant making a wide detour, leaving the river that had been good company for 3,000 miles and subsequently running short of water in a hot and arid land. 'It would not be too fanciful to suggest', I read, 'that during the past two or three thousand years the Sudd has had a profound, though negative, influence on the history of eastern tropical Africa.' It would also not be fanciful to propose that wherever a swamp has occurred to any major degree it has had a powerful influence upon its locality, hindering, detracting, stopping. The tundra is easygoing by comparison; so is a forest, a desert, a mountain or even snow and ice. They are all obstacles but are not the total blockage of a swamp. *Homo sapiens* is an adroit creature on the whole, but he does badly in any stretch of mud. He would be better off, I concluded, looking ruefully at my shirt, if he were a salamander, mottled or otherwise.

This final kind of wilderness is therefore the most obstructive to man as well as being the most vulnerable to his activities. The joint fact helps to explain his determination throughout the ages to proceed with engineering works that swiftly put paid to a swamp. Of course, there is such a scheme for the Sudd: it is called the Jonglei canal. Like all such notions the plan is comprehensive: dig a channel, prevent even floodwater from bursting its banks, slow down evaporation and make a river highway, straight as a reed where reeds will grow no more. This enormous enterprise would cost an astronomical amount. It would also have far-reaching consequences, totally destroying former styles of life. The Nasser Dam, 15° of latitude further north, has produced results that few anticipated (at least out loud): bilharzia increase, fertility loss with the loss of silt, destruction of the delta's pilchard industry. That dam's immense reservoir, drowning such a quantity of land (and burying yet more deeply a great-grandfather of mine who died in the area), evaporates water almost to rival the Sudd, but it produces the blessings of a controlled river and much-needed electricity. The Jonglei scheme would also create advantages and disadvantages. 'What would happen to the Dinkas?' I once asked, having seen these naked giants and their beloved cattle. 'They could not sustain the herds that they possess today if the swamp were all to go.' 'Oh, well,' said a Sudanese, 'they would learn to plant rice instead.'

It was in 1955 that I first encountered the Sudd. At Juba, the capital of Sudan's province of Equatoria, I had learned of this huge barrier lying to the north. 'Better take the steamer,' said someone. 'It's the best way. Only takes nine days. You see, it's downstream going north.' Nine days! Downstream! People cross the Atlantic in less time than that. 'Better take some food,' added my informant, 'unless you want to go first-class, when all meals are provided.' At once, as we were talking loudly on the quayside, I became surrounded with food for sale. Most of it lay down and nibbled hopefully at stones from time to time. Some of it hung down, held by its feet and trying to keep at least its head upright. Supplementing the goats and chickens were all manner of other nourishments heaped upon the earth: millet seed, red-hot chillis, bone-dry fish and bamboo lengths of sugar-cane. My nine days of voyaging would plainly be active, first in converting the food into meals, and then caring for a stomach terribly bombarded with poor cooking and alien offerings. I felt the seed. I chewed a proffered husk of cane. I looked at a goat which looked unblinking back at me. 'Where do I get a ticket?' I said; adding prudently, 'the first-class kind that will provide my meals?'

Those nine days were an extraordinary voyage. Around the central craft, whose stern paddle-wheel thumped both night and day, were all manner of other hulks. Some had been power units in their time. Others were more like barges, flat-bottomed, flat-topped and full of people who behaved as if they were at home. They slept, they made fires upon the steel, cooked, and then they slept again. I saw my goat for a day or two and then no more. Above all, and stretching away on every side, I saw papyrus. Close at hand each mop of bracts moved gently as we passed. Further away they did not move but just stood upon the mud, growing, transpiring, dying and flowering for several thousand square miles.

Our boat, so garlanded with other craft, was not the most nimble of vehicles. Its helmsman, sitting cross-legged by the wheel, would do his best, fling the rudder this way and that, ring down instructions to the hell-house of an engine room, and then watch stoically as we hit the shore again. The Nile's meanderings were often too severe for our turning capabilities; we hit, reversed, stopped, advanced, and hit again a few points further on. With each collision a raft of papyrus would set off downstream and we followed, but such collisions were crucial. Without them, and without those battering passages through the Sudd, it would swiftly regain its former territory. When it seemed to have done so already, when it seemed that we were stuck for good, it was possible to sense again the fearful power of this wilderness. How long would a man survive? A few hours perhaps, if he thrashed wildly in despair, or longer if he stayed silently, accepting defeat from the start. Today, from city outposts, we see wilderness as a kind of friend. More often it is an enemy, something to put us down; and the Sudd would put one down most certainly.

It is such a wilderness that even other forms of life find it hard to flourish there. The trouble with a dominant species, such as papyrus, is that it does not permit a variety of habitats. In consequence, there is a similar lack of different kinds of animal. As we made our way through the forest of papyrus we saw very little else. Occasionally there was a crocodile. Even less frequently there were hippos, submerging as we thrashed by and re-emerging later to stare at the thing which had thundered over them. When a bad corner gripped us, and our paddles churned the water an even muddier brown, terns would appear from nowhere to take advantage of whatever it was we were stirring up for them; but birds, in the main, were a rarity. This in itself was strange. There are probably a thousand species to be found in the harsh land of Sudan, making a living in all kinds of arid areas; but, at the Sudd's centre, however lush it looked, there were fewer individuals than might be seen on an ocean voyage. An infrequent *Balaeniceps rex*, the shoe-billed stork with more of a boot than a shoe by way of a beak. The squacco heron, making a disaster of every landing among the stems. The purple gallinule, the long-toed lily-trotter, goliath heron, finfoot, cormorant—all such birds were far more frequent whenever breaks occurred in the papyrus panoply. So too were fish eagles, geese and plovers; the sight of such creatures in abundance meant we were nearing the end of the Sudd's dominions.

For our film I was excited by the idea that we should sail again from Juba to the north. What better way to invade this wilderness? I described the lavish attendance, the iced sherbet drinks, the frequent meals rich with courses, a mosquito-proof top-deck set high to catch the breeze. Let us not bother, I suggested, with any other travel than the best, the first-class kind. Let us have nine days of wilderness wonder. Let us, in short, go down to the quay again, disregard the goats and millet seed, and choose cabins worthy of a lust for luxury.

So we went down to the wharf. The air was precisely as I remembered it, syrupy soft and hung about with smoke. The sky

162

was as dark when evening came as a tropical sky should be. The Nile gurgled past with the same old energy and undoubtedly the Sudd itself, not many miles downstream, would not have changed just because I had turned my back on it for a score of years. 'What pleasure we will have,' I said. 'Just you wait and see.'

Certainly we waited. We did a lot of that. We also hammered on a door, on several doors. Just where was everybody? And where were all the goats and the scarcely edible foods I remembered so vividly? Come to that, where was the boat?

'Tomorrow,' said an old man who loomed from nowhere in the dark. 'Try tomorrow,' he added, and so we did. We also tried the next day, and it was quite a while before the boat appeared to keep us company.

'There is great hardship in my country,' explained a young man who, in exchange for a bundle of cash, wrote a ticket for us on a page of an exercise book. 'Here is your cabin,' he announced, before filling the air with Arabic and emptying the room of an older man who, amazingly in that turmoil of a turn-round, had been asleep on the bed. 'Have a good journey,' concluded our ticket salesman, using his foot to edge out a pile of rubbish on the floor, 'and do not forget the hardship that we have suffered here.'

How perverse is selfishness! It seemed much easier to contemplate our own plight as we realised how things had changed since the days I so fondly remembered. The cabin gave us an early clue, especially its bed, heavy with the sweat and dirt of previous travellers. So too the fact, learned too late for remedial action, that meals were not as they had been twenty years ago. There were no six-course meals for first-class passengers, no one-course meals, no meals of any kind. We looked nervously at our own resources. They happened to be, as chance would have it, two tins of Wall-of-China Corned Beef, twenty-three bottles of beer and an apple. The voyage had been exceptional all those years before. It looked like being no less remarkable on the second occasion. We opened a bottle from the limited choice, drank a toast to memory and prepared once again, but with fewer perquisites, to enjoy a wilderness.

Wilderness

They say that when Allah made the Sudan Allah laughed, because the top half is a desert and the bottom half a swamp. It was with appropriate levity that we approached the lower part of his handiwork. In doing so we realised that our beef, named after an ancient monument, was correctly tough and our diet rapidly became beer alone, which, in the circumstances, was just as well. The ship, I must confess, was foul. The food, even after we had located, embraced and poured drink into the cook, was wholly lacking. The smoke from the frenzied boilers was more grit than gas, and both would pour down upon our heads each time we ran into yet another bank. Allah may well have laughed at the swamp of his creation, but he must have hysterics watching men try to master it. Certainly we, no longer with the cares of eating and digestion, also viewed the matter fairly buoyantly. It was a crazy, incoherent hallucination of a voyage, and we relished it avidly.

Earlier I bemoaned the fact that airliners give no inkling to their passengers of the land that flows beneath, but other forms of travel are also guilty. To stop a car along a lonely road is suddenly to realise the existence of all sorts of novelties, the smell of the air, and the sound and feel of it. Even to stop a bike is to put an end to its kind of interference. Therefore I was doubly delighted with the passage of our vessel through the Sudd. It did stop, time and again. It went backwards; it sailed broadside on; it became a raft whenever the motors failed; but, even at full speed with not a bend in view, its haste was not unseemly. It was more of a walking pace, more in keeping with a wilderness, faster when the flow was stronger and slower when we idled in a lake. To go through that emptiness with out amalgam of vessels, making a jam of traffic entirely on our own, may appear as the very converse of ideal; but it was just right. No craft more excellent could have been devised for that most splendid of voyages.

Not until the very end of the last century were sufficient journeys made through the Sudd for the waterway to stay cleared. Before then each passage was like the first. With the increase in traffic even papyrus did not have time to cover up the open water created along the route. Therefore, much like feet making and then maintaining a pathway, the steamers were vital; but that was before *Eichhornia* arrived. No one knows who uprooted the South American water hyacinth, admired it, transported it, and then let it loose in the late 1950s upon the continent of Africa; but everyone knows the hurt it caused. It clogs rivers, stops boats, uses oxygen, destroys fish, and creates a kind of havoc that Africa does not need. Unfortunately, the very battering of a boat, particularly if it destroys each blockage on its way, merely distributes the weed. Broken fragments float away, settle elsewhere, grow to clog another place and do great damage. There had been no rival to papyrus when I made my first journey, but there were great acres of *Eichhornia* when I came back to savour the scene again. They were of lesser substance than the thick stems of papyrus, and therefore no real hindrance, but they added to the problems in that blockage of a swamp.

For days we lived upon our boat. It was no faster than before, and the stream ahead no broader; if anything the speed and width had lessened with the years. Our hunger rose to a peak, and then waned with time. The beer expired and even the Wall-of-China beef was attacked; but still the *Mars*, for so our ship was called, thundered northwards (and sideways and backwards) through that endlessness of green. It was a most forbidding wilderness. It was neither water nor land. It was more impassable than snow, rock, ice, forest, sand; it outdid them all. I stared and stared at it, bemused, amazed, delighted and horrified. Like one shipwrecked I lost count of the days. I moved about the decks, climbed ladders, inspected everything and always came back to that same old view, the unending sea of the Sudd.

In time, of course, it ended, and so did the journey. There was a sadness, but I remember well how we hurried ashore, talking of food and little else. Within four hours, having retrieved some baggage items gone astray, we were in a hotel. Within four more a meal was coming our way. The elderly waiter wore sandals, made more vivid in our eyes because leprosy or something similar had eaten much of his toes. He shuffled with difficulty, sniffed with ease, took sauce from an old paint-tin, blew to make the salt run freely, wiped our implements upon an aged cloth and then set a dish before us. It was of fish, first fried and then forgotten. We all looked at it for quite a length of time. Our waiter looked at us and then turned upon his heels, which I saw, had suffered like his toes. They say that hungry men can lose their taste for food. They also say that organs wither with disuse. We chose to say 'Let's go' and so we did. Later, having scoured the town and dined off sugar-cane and another tin of China beef, we were all agreed that fried fish had never been our favourite dish.

Down at the river's edge the White Nile looked just as determined as it had done 300 miles further south. It flowed strongly between its banks, giving no hint that a formidable barrier had—at great price—just been overcome. Like an army that closes ranks and marches as if no slaughter has occurred, the White Nile moved northwards steadily and gave no clue of the Sudd. To the north it collects reinforcements from its union with the Sobat, a large river flowing from the east, and again continues on its way. The next major union is with the Blue Nile at Khartoum. Then, refreshed once more and still heading north, it flows right through the Nubian desert, piles up behind the Nasser Dam and then gives life to Egypt. It is a majestic and wonderful river, the world's longest and, to my mind, the most glamorous. No wonder they had to search for its source and no wonder, knowing the Sudd as we now do, they only found it by going round the back, by starting at Zanzibar rather than Alexandria. Lake Victoria is a fitting starting-place for such a remarkable river, this stream that kept its secret for so long, flowed through lakes and deserts, poured over the Murchison Falls, almost lost itself in the world's largest swamp, but was strong enough to emerge again with only half its substance gone.

'Just how long is this River Nile?' said an Irishman who happened to be standing with us on that final evening. 'Just how long is it (and here he paused) from bank to bank?.

We laughed, and said he should remember the Sudd. 'It's even longer there, about ninety miles in the widest part—from bank to bank.'

Alas, it was our final evening. Afterwards I remember hours in an enclosed transport plane, time in Khartoum, climbing from a hotel at some small hour intending to let the night-watchman continue in his sleep but pulling down a length of rail upon his turbanned head. I remember seeing the vastness of Lake Nasser filling up each cranny of the land as if a flood had come, and then it was Cairo, and then somewhere else, and the Atlantic, and Miami, and Jacksonville, and Folkston, and a signboard that said 'Drive in here for Okefenokee'. I drove straight in.

As with Australia where I began, and as with every other wilderness I had come to see, I could see no point in dallying once I had arrived. They gave me a canoe, threw in a bag of food, handed over a pole and shouted a batch of instructions: 'Head for the Suwannee canal, mind the 'gators, make a left to reach the prairie, and then you're on your own.'

It was good to hear those words as well as the Southern accent that came along with them. 'Then you're on your own,' I said to myself again and again, hoping to capture the cadence and trying to master the boat simultaneously. This is pure sentiment and what I really loved were the implications of that phrase, the situation, the fact of being once again at the start of a wilderness. Being on my own in a new place, and poling a canoe to discover it, is a joy that I find overwhelming. There was again that brink of pain.

As I reached the Suwannee, mastered the craft, poled contentedly and watched my wake reach into the banks, I was suddenly aware of another wake just ahead of me. *Alligator mississippiensis* was acting as guide and escort. Together the pair of us moved forward through that black water, overlooked by cypress trees, flown over by herons and ibises, and blown over by no vestige of a wind. A pair of sandhill cranes went by, two crosses flying through the air. A group of white-tailed deer stared until their courage cracked and they splashed away. And high up in a tree - what a world this is! - there was a family of bears, the parents looking anxious, the young ones quite relaxed. My alligator, never much more than a wake, led me to the turning place and then vanished out of sight. I prodded gingerly with the pole for a few strokes, having no wish to impale my escort, and then turned left as they had instructed one hour earlier.

There you will find the prairie, they had said, and so I did. Instead of trees there was a great expanse with nothing higher than me. In the Sudd I had been dwarfed by nine-foot papyrus but here I towered over everything; acres of water-lilies, pastel-coloured pitcher plants, grasses, reeds, dragonflies, and scores of croaking frogs. In time, swamps being what they are, I could not persuade the flat-bottomed boat, drawing two inches at most, to go further. So, having looked for any 'gators there might be, I stepped overboard and started to haul.

The water was about a foot deep. It was splendidly warm, peat-soft at the bottom, and it bathed my legs in bubbling effervescence. To stand still was to sink slowly, but without alarm, into the peat below. To jump was to sink at once, with considerable alarm, some four feet down. There is so much rotting vegetation, and so much gas along with it, that the peaty platform has risen to the surface. This can support a man provided he does not treat it as a trampoline. The name of Okefenokee means 'trembling earth' in the Seminole tongue, and it does wobble before giving way to leave the visitor chest-high in water and trembling on his own account. He is at that moment eye to eye with any alligator and his limbs are much impeded from taking whatever action he might have in mind. Such as running away. Or walking away. Or just standing on the peaty platform once again.

The boat was all-important. I pulled myself back on board, freeing my legs from the peat, and gazed again at salamander-coloured limbs. It did seem as if the great bogs of the world had this much in common. An osprey flew over, uttered a disdainful cry, and settled on the bare bones of a very ancient tree. Likewise a woodpecker, one of the six species in the area. While drying out I fumbled for the bird book and quickly realised why I had so far failed in naming most of them. There are three kinds of egret, six of heron, two of bittern, nineteen types of duck, three nuthatches and even four vireos. A warbler of a sort flew over as I sat there. I looked up warblers, found there were twenty-six in the area and put the book away. Besides, I had dried out.

When poling the boat along, revelling in a bog that permitted progress of any kind, my principal companions were the alligators. Not that I saw much of them, beyond a flurry in the water and churned-up colour where they had been. The place would boil

168

briefly and then a streak of peaty-brown would mark where the animal had sped away. To see one properly it was best to halt and then look carefully at every likely place. Nine out of ten would be unoccupied but the final one, a spot where some reeds hung gently from above, would have a lump of black that was somehow alien. It did not move but it had a sheen that, once seen, was distinctly memorable. The eyes were the greatest give-away, despite the slit of a pupil and the unblinking stare. As I became more adept at detecting these repriles around me I was amazed at their quantity. Once (and that was enough) I even put the pole on one before, with a mighty flourish, it had me overboard. I have no idea where the animal went and even less about my own passage in these moments. Later, I concluded it was the parula warbler I had seen earlier as, perusing the book, I quietly dried again.

In time, having poled some more, I came across a nest. A gardener would call it a compost heap, and he would be right in a way; but for the alligator it is a nest, warm in its decomposition and just right for hatching eggs. The female makes it and, essentially, it is no more than a pile of vegetation, reaching four feet above the water-line. Around this is a cleared area, making the heap resemble a mound of food upon a plate, and through this open area I punted cautiously. Apparently the female always guards her nest but not obtrusively. She does not lie, as dragons did, across her precious possessions, but lurks elsewhere ready to chase off raccoons if need be, bears if possible but never, so I had learned, a human visitor. Nevertheless, I looked around carefully, saw nothing, stepped slowly into the water, and waded to the nest. Out of curiosity I plunged an arm into that compost heap. It was warm and thick but, about fifteen inches down, I came across the eggs and pulled one out. It was two inches long, one inch wide and therefore more oval than most eggs. It was also differentially coloured, one half pinker than the other, but I almost dropped it when my boat chose on its own to drift my way. From the corner of an eye I felt my hour had come. Unnerved (even though it was just the boat), I replaced the egg with haste, smoothed the disturbance, climbed on board, picked up the pole and punted through the prairie with an energy I had not noticed earlier.

That evening, surrounded by a great deal of drawling southern talk, I asked how the swamp had managed to survive. Admittedly it was not a big wilderness, not in the league of others on my tour, but it was twenty-five miles across and its 400,000 acres had, I felt sure, been coveted in the past. Moreover, the state of Georgia was not some distant outpost but one of the original thirteen colonies, founded by charter in 1732 and actively developed long before that time. There must have been ample opportunity and desire to transform these 600 square miles of Georgia swamp into 600 square miles of land. So how had it survived?

'We-ll, I reckon it was mainly luck. In fact, if you ask me, I'd go further than that 'cos I reckon it was luck all along the line.' The others also reckoned that he was about right on, hitting it fair and square, nailing it plumb central, telling it like it was and like it should be told. Thereafter, between the mint juleps and the pecan pie, I learned more about that luck.

Even in the eighteenth century there had been a plan to drive a canal through Georgia and Florida that would have permitted vessels to sail a short cut from the Atlantic to the Gulf of Mexico. The plan, had it not been too ambitious for its day (with Florida still foreign territory), would also have taken care of the Oke swamp. In the nineteenth century, when good Indians were dead Indians (although this remark was not attributed to anyone in particular until 1869), a few local groups took refuge in the swamp. There was a plan to drain the area and destroy their hiding-place, but the Indians moved further south and the swamp's acres were once again reprieved. Agriculture then became the motive, although such peaty soil would make poor fields, and an engineer was hired to drain the place. At great expense he dug the Suwannee Canal (along which I had poled with such delight) but, as he discovered too late, he had made it on the wrong side of the swamp: the canal brought water into the area rather than out of it. It is easy to jeer at the error, but it is also very easy to be relieved. Finally, the timber men moved in, put down railway lines, cut down the worthwhile cypress trees and then, that done,

170

took out the lines along with the last of the logs. Silence descended again.

'That was all yesterday,' said my host. 'Yup, that's all gone by. But now we've got today. We've got problems raining now that make those of yesterday no more than heavy dew.' There are times when I look at my notebook with disbelief but, mint juleps or no, that is what it says he said. It seems that everyone is wanting a bit of the swamp. The tourists want all of it, for canoe trails, air-boat rides, boardwalks, trailer parks, boat rentals. Fishermen cannot wait to get at the bass, bluegill, warmouth, catfish and pickerel. Hunters wish to hunt. Motel and all manner of other operators want to build, on stilts if need be, so that all who come can see 'famed Okefenokee, haunt of 'gators, inspiration of Stephen C. Foster' (who never came near the place although he wrote 'Swannee River'), 'home of Chief Billy Bowlegs, leader of the warring Seminoles'. A Disneyland has been proposed. So too a further cropping of the cypresses now they have grown again (although they take a thousand years to reach old age), and an extension of the turpentine business, which taps trees for their resin, such trees growing well in swampy areas. 'Sure we got problems,' went on my host; 'never been short of them. But right now we've got a respite, and you won't never guess how we got it.'

He was right. I didn't guess, but I was delighted with the story. There were so many claimants to the swamp, all proposing splendid benefits for the local community, that their respective cases had to be publicly heard. It was decided to have a mass hearing rather than a series of individual applications. So, at this meeting, each spokesman for each cause had his turn, made his plea and then sat silently while lesser causes were proclaimed. The final speaker had been saved, or so I was led to suspect, until the end because his case was so awful and so monstrous in its implications that it would stun the audience.

'I propose', this man then said, 'to create a scenic route right through the very centre of this swamp. People will see it from their very own cars, and the new highway will cut driving time from New York City to the State of Florida by a substantial quantity.' He sat down. Whoever had stage-managed the order of events must have held his breath, but he had been right. People were incredulous. There were murmurings at first, and then talk, loud talk, outspoken and angry talk at the very idea. It was vehemently denounced, ruled out of order, condemned entirely. In fact, as the manager had suspected all along, it was castigated so violently that every other proposal was dismissed as well. Not a single suggestion, however promising, stood a chance once that meeting's wrath had been roused. A scenic route! Right through the centre! What a thought! Besides, as everyone had somehow learned, its proposer was a man from quite another town.

Nevertheless, there have been concessions. I personally think they have been wise and the more I looked at this refuge of a swamp, despite its muddled history and its current complex ownership (American administration of such areas can entangle a newcomer as effectively as any bog), the more I liked its style. Basically, it was in three parts, the first being the most frightening and, in its way, the most cunning.

I encountered it when still punting on my own. Where there had been tranquillity there was suddenly a crowd. Fibreglass boats, packed with people and powered by electric outboards, were being driven at quite a speed by young men who, throughout the twenty minute trip, would regale each boat-load with swamp stories and swamp data and point out passing happenings. An old still, left in place from the bootlegging era, would be sited on the left. On the right would be a group of deer, grazing casually, having seen such visitors before and knowing, even if the visitors did not, that green chain-link fencing kept them firmly in that section. An alligator is resting upon a bank, and a nest is round a corner further on. There is then a pause, occasion for a story from the past, of crooks and Indians, of 'gator hunters who made a living in the place. Soon on again, past low hanging moss, the elbow stumps grown by cypress trees at the water-line, a woodpecker hole high up, a bear print on the ground. Finally, back to the jetty where the tour started and where the tickets are sold for 'a swamp experience'. The place also sells much more—alligator souvenirs, cypress table-mats, presents from Okefenokee, State of Georgia.

It is easy to mock, but the idea should not be mocked. It is a pressure valve, taking the heat off 99 per cent of the swamp's domain, giving people a taste of the place, doing it profitably and giving them much of what they want. It too has been stage-managed carefully. What is the point of alligator country if there are no alligators in view? So people leave the boat feeling they have had their money's worth, the trip had been a good choice, they were fortunate in their guide and lucky in the sights that came to pass. They should never, I believe, be prevented from seeing such sights, or feel frustrated. They should drive away happy, ready to recommend the tour to friends, and in the main they probably did. The pressure valve was doing its job most effectively.

However, there are also other kinds of people, those who want to linger longer, go their own way and take time in doing so. Their wishes too have been considered. They can hire boats or use their own provided the engine is not above 10 h.p. Then, suitably equipped with maps, information and injunctions about litter, they can set off, camp if they wish at designated spots and live for a while in a kind of wilderness. Once again the stage-managing has been performed with appropriate aplomb. For example, it is difficult, as I had already learned, to make progress through a swamp. With a propeller clogging itself in the water-lilies, it can be harder still. Therefore the authorities, using a sort of flail, have arranged some casual waterways that look entirely natural. There are even signposts but these do not offend. There are also lavatories, a novelty for a wilderness, set within clumps of trees. These do not disfigure. They are practical and, however foreign to the scene, can serve the area more wholesomely than natural alternatives.

What the visitor does not realise is that his journeying has been arranged, keeping him firmly out of at least half of this wilderness; but he or she is no less ecstatic for that unknown denial. There is more than enough to see, to experience, to gaze and wonder at. I saw a woman extracting herself from her canoe and bubbling with joy at the days she had just spent. 'Oh Mr Hopkins,' she called out, 'It's wonderful. It all reminds me so much of something I have never seen.' Out came my book and I wrote down at once.

The third part of Okefenokee is the most exciting. This half that the visitors cannot see is sacrosanct. Nobody goes there. Certainly the twenty-minute tourists come nowhere near this area. Nor do the individualists paddling their own canoes. Nor do fishermen who, after acquiring licences, can go their lonely ways. Nor even scientists, who tend to think that wilder places are reserved for them, or ought to be. I liked this idea of a reservation, strictly for nature. I would not see it, of course, but I liked the idea of it being there, a place where people cannot go. It is not impossible to reach, impenetrable or even unwelcoming. It is just that, at long last, people have made a rule that will keep people out. Only nature on her own will flourish there.

On my final day I went into the cypress groves. I had seen the occasional tree but not that part of the swamp where they dominate, standing in the water as thickly as a forest stands upon the land. The water there is very black, stained by tannin seeping into it. The lack of wind is also a feature and the reflections can be as perfect as in glass. Punting is not possible, with the branches hanging down, but paddling is feasible. There is no need for pathways here, because there are no banks of peat, no prairie acres of lily fields, but just the silence of the trees, heavy with their moss. It was a most delectable spot.

Somewhere there were those package tours, chancing upon their static animals. Somewhere else there were fishermen, and ornithologists, and scientists, and weekenders far from home. I myself was on my own, a little lost, I recollect, but most contented with my lot. I put the paddle on one side, lay back, looked at the patterns up above and drank in this further wilderness. I listened to its silences and heard the noises speckled in between. I watched the sun sprinkling through the leaves. I felt at peace. This was enchantment at the centre of a swamp. It was isolation and a union with the world of natural things. Then I remembered that other emptiness, the part of the swamp where no one goes, the half that is for nature on its own. This remembrance abruptly made my part better still.

8 *The Wilderness Ideal*

> Man is tinkering with his environment; and the absolute requirement of intelligent tinkering is to save all the parts.
> *Aldo Leopold*

Americans are more perturbed about the concept of wilderness than the people of any other nation, in part because of the pace at which things happened there. Europe has also suffered change but, in terms of wilderness destruction, it has been almost at a standstill for the past two thousand years. Its huge emptinesses had vanished earlier. The most recent estimate of England's rural population when the Romans came is 5 million, or half the number that live in England's countryside today. In consequence, Europeans do not feel that wilderness is a recent loss: the bulk of it had gone so very long ago. Not in America.

Subduing the new world was a colossal task, whether or not anyone stopped to consider it. Imagine being an early colonist, informed of the vastness of the new dominion, of its 100 per cent of wilderness, and then being told to tame the place without delay, cut down its forests, destroy its indigenous tribes, make roads, farms, fields, towns. Prepare the ground for 200 million people. Wire it up for electricity, telephones. Find water for everyone. Discover the minerals and dig them up. Make airports, factories; make it the biggest industrial complex there has ever been. And do the job, not over millennia as a neolithic pace of life merges into modern times, but in the three and a half centuries from the Pilgrims to today. The land area exceeds two thousand million acres but the task was tackled with such zest that, by the end of the allotted time, only 2 per cent of its original wilderness still remained.

'The onslaught of the 19th century on the forests of North America was so shocking that [it] was the reason for the early rise of their sense of conservation,' wrote Frank Fraser Darling. 'One of the most startling realisations . . . was the almost sudden awareness that there are no areas available for preservation as wilderness which are not already devoted to some other purpose,' wrote Howard Zahniser slightly earlier. [He largely wrote the Wilderness bill—see page 180—but died just before its victory.] Divide the current population of the United States into that part of the land still classifiable as wilderness, and the result is a quarter of an acre for each American of today. The colonists of the new world did an extraordinary job of subjugation and only recently have their descendants realised what it is that they have done. Consequently, American thinking now on the subject of wilderness is both apposite and instructional. There are many sound statements but also, to my mind, a kind of eco-baloney unmatched elsewhere. In a page or two I shall look at the new plans, and marvel at some of the statements made; but, until then, it is important to reflect upon earlier mankind, what it thought of wilderness and what a change of heart has come to pass.

There were about 500 million people on this planet when the age of exploration began. The bulk of them were on the three old continents, Europe, Asia and Africa, totalling 32 million square miles. The old land was not particularly crowded (more than six times as many lives are being lived on it today) but the explorers came from Europe and that continent was, in general, the most crowded of the three. It was Europeans who discovered the vast new lands. They circled Africa. They found the Americas, although it took them time to comprehend their size. That done, they searched for Terra Australis, presumed to exist as counterweight to all the northern land and because, so some alleged, the space down there just had to contain a continent. They did not find as much southern land as had been suggested, but Australia is 3 million square miles and sixty times bigger than England, the country that took care of it. This new place therefore helped to relieve any sensation of population pressure that might have been welling at the time. At last there came the discovery of the final continent, desperately inhospitable but another 5 million square miles to be drawn upon the map.

The age of discovery also began just when people were comprehending that they stood on a finite planet. Such an understanding should have been restrictive but, due to those discoveries, the very converse was the case. Spain, Portugal, England, Holland, France—they were small countries compared to the enormous tracts they were naming as their own. Brazil is almost a hundred times the size of Portugal. Spain had the other half of South America, plus a great deal more lying to the north. France and Britain were competing for Canada, a piece of land twelve times their combined size but just one morsel of the huge meal the two of them attacked. In other words the planet was suddenly finite in its area and simultaneously enormous in its possibilities.

This contradiction is neatly demonstrated by an act of the Spanish royal house. For centuries it had been proud of its situation at the western end of the Mediterranean. It guarded the Pillars of Hercules (the Straits of Gibraltar) which marked the end of the known world. The royal family's *impresa* had, as its motto, *Ne Plus Ultra*—there is no more beyond. When Columbus dramatically upset this applecart, and Spain busily discovered new fruits for herself, the insignia was plainly wrong. Some unsung hero put forward a brilliant proposal. *Plus Ultra* then became the Spanish motto—more is beyond. This change occurred when, to borrow a phrase and concept from Peter Medawar, man became a 'biological success'. There was suddenly no stopping him. In numbers he was climbing from a base line where he had stayed for so long. He was taking off just at the very moment when he was discovering another half of the planet on which to exercise himself—a half that was steeped in wilderness.

Wilderness

The history of the United States parallels this global story. As soon as pressures began to build up something happened to refresh the old idea of more and more beyond. Naturally the earliest colonists could see no frontiers to their vast new land. When restrictions from home grew oppressive they won their independence, liberating their thoughts yet again. Then came the Louisiana Purchase which, for mere money, more than doubled the area of the new United States. Afterwards came wars with Mexico, when Texas, New Mexico and southern California were all acquired. Steadily more stars were added to the stripes: Colorado, Washington, Montana, Idaho, Wyoming, Oklahoma. How could anyone contemplate compression when there was always more at hand? Besides, there were world wars to worry about, and after them the United States could relax as the most powerful nation anywhere on earth.

Then came trauma. Some people have dated it as precisely as 1957 (or thirteen generations after the Pilgrim Fathers set out). There had been murmurings beforehand, the establishment of national parks (starting with Yellowstone in 1872) and pronouncements from proto-conservationists; but there had not been a national outcry, a new fury by all sorts and kinds of men. Quite suddenly Henry David Thoreau, dead for almost a century, writer of two books, arch-defender of nature, idleness and other lonely causes, came into his own. A prophet had been crying in the wilderness, and people rushed to read him. In Thoreau's proclamations they found the slogans of which America felt in need. 'What is the use of a house', he had written all those years before, 'if you haven't got a tolerable planet to put it on?' What indeed! everyone cried. What wisdom he had had to have seen it all so plainly even before it had occurred!

'Conservation replaced motherhood', wrote Paul Brooks, 'as the safest thing to be for.' All manner of arguments were used, all kinds of sources. Someone remembered Job: 'Ask now the beasts and they shall teach thee; and the fowls of the air, and they shall teach thee.' And Benjamin Rush: 'Man is naturally a wild animal . . . taken from the woods, he is never happy . . . till he returns to them again.' And Ralph Waldo Emerson: 'Nature is the

178

incarnation of thought . . . In the woods we return to reason and faith.' There was humility at the loss, and also desperation. So much had gone; so little remained. Not only the trees and wildness had disappeared, but virtues far harder to define. 'We are exterminating half the basis of English poetry,' cried Aldous Huxley. 'When man obliterates wilderness', wrote the physicist J. A. Rush, 'he repudiates the evolutionary force that put him on this planet. In a deeply terrifying sense, man is on his own.' 'The real significance of wilderness is a cultural matter,' wrote Sigurd Olson, '. . . And what we are trying to conserve is not scenery as much as the human spirit itself.'

On more practical terms the wilderness was said to be a base datum of normality, a laboratory for the study of land health, a genetic resource, a supplier of medicines (50 per cent of current US prescription ingredients are derived from nature). It was called the stabilising force of the planet, the one eternal blessing. There were frightening prophecies about melting ice, axing Amazonia, making CO_2; but, judging from statements proclaimed in recent years, it is not these practical fears that have created most alarm. It is the wilderness *idea*, the wilderness *concept*, the fact of something disappearing which is favoured but scarcely understood. Wallace Stegner, another American conservationist, summed up this enigma: 'Being an intangible and spiritual resource, it will seem mystical to the practical-minded—but then anything that cannot be moved by a bulldozer is mystical to them.'

Hand in hand with these remarks were others of less appeal. It was affirmed that Thoreau could get more out of ten minutes with a woodchuck than others could from a night with Cleopatra. Theodore Roszak, the new messiah—for some—said he hoped ecology would be a replacement for scientific analysis and provide 'a new science in which the object of knowledge will be rather like the poet's beloved: something to be contemplated but not analysed, something . . . permitted to retain its mysteries'. In that case the substitute for scientific analysis will scarcely stem from ecology which, to my mind, happily attempts to dispel mysteries and destroys none of the wonder in doing so. Primitive man, wrote

179

a promoter of the wilderness cause, 'saw and experienced the world as a web of intricate interrelationships of which he, in common with every other living thing—everything indeed in nature—was an inseparable and connected part'. Did he really? Did he not heave a rock if he saw something good to eat? The Duke of Wellington expressed disquiet over the troops on his side, and hoped they would frighten the enemy as much as they frightened him. We must all sympathise with that view from time to time.

Nevertheless, however varied the bedfellows who spoke out on behalf of wilderness, they were sufficiently united to cause a great leap forward in conservational legislation. It was on 3 September 1964 that, in the Rose Garden of the White House, as suitable a setting as any in the area, President Lyndon Johnson signed the Wilderness Act. This established the National Wilderness Pre-servation System and made the United States the first country to proclaim through law a recognition of wilderness in its way of life. The Act had had a difficult passage. Timber, oil, grazing and mining industries had been against it, stating that resources were meant to be used and not admired. ('You can't eat scenery' was a famous remark of the time.) The National Park Service and the Forest Service, two federal agencies firmly involved, had also opposed it in its early days. There were eighteen separate public hearings. The bill was rewritten again and again. It was passed in the Senate and then held up in the House of Representatives. There were eight years of discussion. Then at last came the day in the Rose Garden when the President signed his name.

The first moves had been made thirty years earlier. Robert Marshall, pioneer of the wilderness idea, had sent a number of notes on the subject to the Secretary of the Interior, and these are now recognised as the opening moves, the Fort Sumter of this particular war. The Wilderness Society (of America), a forthright protagonist in the campaign to come, was also created at this time. However, at first the fuse burned slowly. There was the Second World War, the cold war, and the Korean War before, abrupt as the craze for hula-hoops, there came the battle for wilderness. It erupted in 1957 and, with something of the energy that had

180

destroyed the land, men set about creating legislation that might safeguard the remainder.

A preamble to the Act of 1964 declares it to be 'the policy of the Congress to secure for the American people of present and future generations the benefits of an enduring resource of wilderness'; but the clause defining that resource provoked the most argument. Here it is in full:

> A wilderness, in contrast with those areas where man and his own works dominate the landscape, is hereby recognised as an area where the earth and its community of life are untrammelled by man, where man himself is a visitor who does not remain. An area of wilderness is further defined to mean in this Act an area of undeveloped Federal land retaining its primeval character and influence, without permanent improvements or human habitations, which is protected and managed so as to preserve its natural conditions and which:
> 1. generally appears to have been affected primarily by the forces of nature, with the imprint of man's work substantially unnoticeable;
> 2. has outstanding opportunities for solitude or a primitive and unconfined type of recreation;
> 3. has at least 5,000 acres of land or is of sufficient size as to make practicable its preservation and use in an unimpaired condition; and
> 4. may also contain ecological, geological, or other features of scientific, educational, scenic, or historical value.

All acts have a fundamental intent which is then eroded by specific provisions. The Wilderness Act, so clean in its definition of empty areas, was equally clear-cut in its basic intent. The regions involved (such as the 54 national forest areas—9·1 million acres) would have: no commercial enterprise, no permanent road (except to meet minimum requirements for administration), no temporary road, no use of motor vehicles, motorised equipment or motorboats, no landing of aircraft, no other form of mechanical transport, and no structure or installation. Unfortunately, eroding that intent, came a string of provisions. There could be aircraft and motorboats if already established. There could be measures to control fire, insects and diseases. There could even be prospecting, providing it was conducted in a manner 'consistent with the concept of wilderness preservation'; and—as the biggest concession of all—there could be 'exploring, drilling, mining and processing operations' until 1 January 1984. Thereafter, irritating the miners but relieving everyone else, only claims existing on that date would stand a chance of approval.

The exemptions sound alarming. A hiker seeking solitude in a wilderness area, who encounters administrative roads, aircraft, pest controllers, fire look-out systems, prospectors and even mines, could well hurry back to his city for a little peace and quiet. The Wilderness Act is not an ideal piece of legislation. It has also not established an ideal wilderness, partly because no one is agreed over what is the ideal. Should fires rage? Should the injured be left to struggle out? Should administration be zero and, if so, how will anyone ensure that the wilderness rules (no machines, no structures, no commercial enterprises) are not being flouted? The Act is a compromise; alas, it had to be; but it is the world's first attempt to keep emptiness firmly on the map. It is imperfect but better than anything in existence before it became law.

Of necessity it is piecemeal. For the visiting Martian and myself, now both accustomed to seeing the enormous wild areas that still remain on Earth, there is a pathetic ring to much of the Wilderness Act. Five thousand acres as a minimum quantity! That is just four miles by two, the size of a small town. What can such a patch hope to give of the feel and scope of wilderness? It is also easy to suspect that many of the wild American areas have only experienced a change in name. 'I was to learn later in life that we tend to meet any new situation by reorganisation, and a wonderful method it can be for creating the illusion of progress,' said one who had plainly suffered from the business of changing names. He was not involved in wilderness, having lived when causes were different, for Caius Petronius had been born at the time of Christ.

Nevertheless, any churlishness on my part, scoffing at the minimum size and quoting from ancient Rome, does not lessen my respect for the Wilderness Act of 1964. It was a sound move. It did represent a change of heart. It will guide others, despite its drawbacks, and will be better still after 1984. (Yellowstone Park was more or less a disaster from its inception in 1872 until 1916 when more money and positive management came its way.) The new Act not only helps to conserve the land and plants and animals (for without them, as has been said, land is mere scenery) but helps us to understand what we want from emptiness.

Certainly it helped me. I began to see wilderness primarily as an absence of restriction. To walk on this earth now is normally to be set about with human barriers. I hated the day when my son first asked if he was allowed to run on a certain stretch of grass. I hate it when I feel hemmed in, by signboards, by statements of ownership. No one yet owns the air or the sea but they do own land and they say so trenchantly. Even community organisations, presumed to exist for the good of all, proclaim their tenure of the land. They call us the public. They give us instructions where to go and what to do. They even lecture about our safety as if that were their affair. In the places where we live we can feel most unwanted and certainly constricted. Every crystal ball, of whatever political colour, will show that such restraint is on the increase. There is no sign of slackening control.

In the countryside this is no less true and can jar more painfully. One child falls over a cliff; so a great fence goes up, hindering a recurrence perhaps, but emphatically destroying the nature of the place. A rare bird nests and people are then kept from it, ornithologists having power and mere people rather less. A pot-holer becomes entrapped and is rescued by other human moles, but not before a cry has risen that such activity should be stopped. It is very easy to be conscious of those who administer many of our empty areas, to learn of their wishes. We are reminded of that ultimate in restrictive notices seen at certain governmental sites: 'Everything which is not expressly permitted is forbidden.'

Upon reflection, my greatest and most singular joy in wilderness was this absence of restraint. The places were too large, too impoverished, too unpleasant for there to be signs of administration. A cliff was a cliff, and I was free to tumble down it any way I chose. Predators were at large, and so was I. My person, as I said in Chapter 1, was again and again a part of the system and no longer its spectator. Nothing had been arranged for my benefit or for my restraint. 'Wilderness is a physical condition,' said Eivind Svoyen, of the National Park Service; 'it is also a state of mind.' How I agree; but time is necessary to reach that state. At the start of each journey into wilderness, when still clutching my boarding-card from the final aeroplane and full of thoughts about man-made things like money, permits or official obstacles, there had to be a jolt to make me realise I was again in wilderness. It could be a polar bear. Or being lost. Or having a snake strike, as one once did, when I stood alone and far from home; but it hit my boot instead of me. I could then enter that other state of mind, revel in it once again, see things differently, forget all ordinary cares, and sense my planet in its reality.

It helped to be alone. There are soul-mates, but to be accompanied is to be communal. To be single is (for me) to admit more emotions, to accept more consequences. It is pleasant not to be alone, but there is then a share-out of reaction to any stimulus. To be lost when single is quite different from being lost in company. To see a wonder, and to have no one nearby who can help absorb the shock, is to be helplessly infused with it from top to toe. Horrors, such as ghosts, appear to those who are on their own. So, I believe, do their opposites, the catchings of breath, the joys that cannot be expressed. Wilderness is a great place for finding solitude and it should never be confused with loneliness.

It would be handy if there were a unit of pleasure, some finite way of measuring happiness. (On the nearby topic of beauty, also short of useful yardsticks, a claim was once made for the milli-Helen, or sufficient beauty to launch one ship.) If there were such a pleasure measurement, the wilderness kept on providing days for me rich in that respect. The happiness of going my own way, making mistakes, finding things and losing track of normal concerns, was a hundred times greater than when others were with me. Discovering a nest is more rewarding than being shown ten of them. To be one of fifty people taken to a site is to experience a certain degree of pleasure. To wander on one's own in that same spot may well cause more delight than the combined pleasure experienced by all the group. There is a similar difference between a child being told a fact and the wonder when that child discovers the same truth for himself.

So what did I learn out there in the wilderness? Was it just, as Robert Frank proposed, that: 'They would not find me changed from him they knew, only more sure of all I thought was true?' I did change. I do see things differently and I will try to explain. H. G. Wells said that reading Bernard Shaw's prefaces was the price to be paid for liking Shaw's plays. If there has been any enjoyment in this book thus far, in being taken by my hand through some of the empty places left on earth, that price must now be paid.

Firstly, I was delighted to realise how much of this planet is still genuinely unscathed, and I have tried to pass on my surprise at this discovery. In the main we live in cities, travel to other cities, keep to the crowded zones and never see or experience the vast and empty areas. We should know that they are there. We should comprehend that fact and feel refreshed by it. There is 70 per cent of our land that will never be touched by agriculture. There is the ice, the tundra; there are the mountains and the deserts; there is much emptiness. We have not destroyed it all, not by any means. The planet Earth, from the Martian's point of view, is still in the main a wild and natural place. This fact should not lessen our new vigilance in wishing to conserve, but it should give comfort that our destruction is not so absolute as many loudly claim. There are great lungs out there, breathing spaces that can give relief however distant they may be. We do not and cannot wander, by and large, as I did from pole to pole. However, we can all think of these places, see on the map that they exist, relish that knowledge, take delight in their presence, know that mankind's tinkering does not obtrude into every single place. A man once wrote that he had never seen the blue whale, and never would see one, but he was delighted that he shared his planet with them. I only saw a minute part of Antarctica, a piece of the tundra here and there, a fragment of other areas; but I am delighted to learn how much they exist—huge, forbidding, dangerous, all nature on her own.

Secondly, there was the joy of being unadministered. Already mentioned, it merits underlining. Human stricture cannot be compared with wild and natural obstacles. There is no malice in them, no offensive authority. A friend of mine, now bitten by a leopard, gored by a hippo, short of the finger struck by a puff adder, is often asked if he got the beasts that got him. Those who put this question are unlikely to understand these paragraphs of

mine. There is not a contest between man and animal. They bite
or strike if there is cause, just as a tree or rock will fall.

Wilderness administrators must tread softly, I believe, if they
are both to do their job and preserve that absence of restraint.
Such men already exist for the newly legislated empty lands of
North America. They exist, even if they have neither seen nor
influenced their huge dominions, for all the big and empty zones.
There is always someone somewhere who is in charge. The US Act
of 1964, so much a pioneer, classified a wilderness but was vague
on management. The new officials are pointing up its weaknesses
by their conflicting plans. Some want to make lakes (enhancing
scenery, spreading public impact), to build tramways (reducing
path damage), to permit cable-cars (what better way to get up or
down a canyon?). Others wish to reduce horse parties, insisting on
no more than (say) six at a time. Some wish to ban the animal
altogether because its feet do more damage than human feet and
it requires different food. Should it be forbidden natural forage,
permitted only imported feed? What if this contains the seeds of
species alien to the area? There is a demand that all horse feed
should be 'pelletised', certified free of foreign seeds, and animals
should be hobbled at night rather than picketed which can lead to
scarred trees and trampled undergrowth. The camp-fire is in
jeopardy. It too can harm the natural scene, as the place is picked
clean of fallen wood. Portable stoves are being recommended in its
stead. Smoking while riding or hiking is being prohibited. Large
parties are required to carry water containers, shovels, axes (with at
least a 2-lb. head and a 26-inch handle), plus survival kits of
whistles, mirrors, waterproof matches, candles, bouillon, sugar, tea,
knives. There are injunctions not to burn or even bury refuse, not to
wash in any stream, and not to stroll away from a filed itinerary.

It is easy to see a manager's point of view. A string of ninety
horses, with people and pack animals, can go through a wilderness
as Thoreau is quoted for all he is worth and a trail is left as from a
regiment on the march. What if the travellers start a forest fire? Or
suffer injury or sickness? My belief is that a diligent manager,
caring for his kingdom, can prevent visitors from experiencing
those very qualities that I hold most dear. If the rules are

obtrusive, and the rulers are not gentle in their ways, those who come to see a wilderness might as well be in a park.

My third realisation was that the size of a wilderness should never be ridiculed. Some are colossal but the visitor is only standing in a part of them and this part, bounded by the horizons that the visitor can see, may be very small indeed. As in a forest; as in a swamp, a thicket, or any place where the view is minimal. The prerequisite is neglect. It must be natural and only man can make it otherwise. They did not, alas, come with me on my tour, but I have been much influenced by my children. We live in London and often drive to other areas; never, of course, to wilderness but frequently to places that are wild in southern England's terms. On arrival I release them from the car and they react accordingly. If it is a managed place, replete with cut grass, notices and other signs of laws, they restrain themselves and wait for me to lumber after them. If it is wild, and apparently unloved, they love it instantly. They rush, leap, find things, see flowers, point out delights, touch bark, hide, and it makes me weep to watch. I may know there is a factory just a belt of trees away, and they may know for all I know; but they do not care. In their way they have found a wilderness, however pocket-sized. Immediately and most expressively, they are pointing up those very virtues that I have been trying to list within the pages of this book.

The sense of freedom is always crucial. Once, to satisfy our curiosity about the British coastline, a group of friends and I travelled right along it, seeing every part of its 6,000 splendid miles. Sometimes the beach and dunes were wide, giving no hint of things inland. Sometimes there was no more than rock, or pebbles, or chalk; but always there was the sea, creeping closer twice a day, hinting with its debris at another world beneath the waves. Each beach seems to have its devotees, and three-quarters of British holidays are spent within sight and sound of the sea. It is colder there, and windier, crowded and expensive, but I believe we love it partly for its taste of wilderness. Children know this fact at once. There are no laws upon the beach. It is wild, natural, refreshed with every tide, and a great place for discovery, injury, observation, energy. It creates a zest for life.

Wilderness

The pace of wilderness is welcomingly natural. My fourth point
is that we, as human beings, can be a part of it. The statement is
often made that primitive man, our ancestor, was hard put to
make ends meet. I do not believe this assertion. I believe, in
general, that only a minor part of his time was passed in acquiring
the needs of life—food, shelter, warmth. He did not stockpile; he
could not. Therefore normal years must have been good years. If
not, the bad years would have been utterly disastrous, killing every
one of his group. Early man must have been able, in the main, to
survive the difficult periods, the one year in ten of drought or
other abnormality. In those times he would have been hungry,
spending more hours each day looking for food, becoming thinner
but, nevertheless, surviving. The normal years must, by this
argument, have been easy years, relatively well provided with basic
needs, leaving ample time for other pursuits, like religion, ritual,
disfigurement, art and other artifice which so fascinate the
anthropologists.

I think it highly abnormal for man to labour as much as he does
in the modern world. There is talk of the leisure problem, as if we
are not innately idle. There is doubt that we could fill our time if
our work (or a major part of it) was taken from us. We are so well
accustomed to it that we rush at our holidays with the same
momentum, seeing this, doing that, travelling to occupy the time.
The man-made kinds of countryside encourage this activity: fish
the lake, hire a boat, reach the café on the hill, visit the ruins, taste
the local produce, buy the curios. A wilderness can, or should,
diminish such fervour. It is not a matter of stopping and staring,
but of slowing down and not looking with any particular purpose
in mind. If the day is warm, sit beneath a tree. If the stones look
agreeable, find the most pleasing of them. It is a wholly different
world from the one that we have made. It is, as life-long conservationist Aldo Leopold remarked, 'the raw material out of
which man has hammered the artefact called civilisation'. There is
no need to hammer at it all over again. Let us take its time.

In a sense my hurtling about the globe, flicking from place to
place, was the very opposite of gentle indolence; but it had a final
compensation. It made me more of a planetary individual. I began

to appreciate that, however ludicrous the concept, I was on a rotating ball in space, girdled by one moon and kept alive by the warmth of a single sun. As the monsoon hit me, or winter darkness the day after equatorial heat, I gradually absorbed the fact of being on a sphere. Once, when flying from Alaska via the great circle that leads to Europe, I asked for a map to help me guess where the sun might rise. Apparently there was no such thing on board, no globe, and I had to make do with an apple. I carved continents on its skin, and in due course the sun rose over my left shoulder. I continued sitting there, pondering on this extra evidence, wondering where the sun might subsequently set, and when. One movie, two meals, three drinks and four apples later it vanished beneath the horizon and, for the record, did so over the same left shoulder. I needed the rest of the journey to discover whether I should warn my fellow passengers and crew of a dramatic shift in the affairs of the universe—or not. It *is* odd being on a planet, and flying north-east from Anchorage to reach Copenhagen lying further to the south, but we need such jolts to bring home to us the extraordinary truth of where we stand.

These, then, scattered through the preceding pages, are my principles. Relish the fact of wilderness. Do not try to tame it. Let it be. Welcome this idea. Become a spectator. Diminish ownership. Restrict restrictions, or impose them cunningly. Remember the joy that children have in any piece of wilderness. Appreciate that it is an idea as much as a place. Know that it is not a commodity belonging to us; it is a community to which we belong. Treasure the ideal of wilderness. Comprehend the planet. Know that it existed, rich in nature, long before us and was impassive to our coming. We have taken charge but, at least in the empty areas, we must strive to lessen our control. Someone said that man should pass like the shadow of a cloud across what he did not make and cannot improve. We are too heavy-footed for such an ideal, but it is worth remembering all the same.

In writing these wishes, and in trying to clarify my thoughts after girdling the earth, a previous experience of delight came to mind. I began to realise, as I listed my ideals for a wilderness, that I had already been to such a place. It had given me more pleasure at the time than all the parks of Africa, and only now could I understand why this had been the case. In its unique manner it had been what I would call a paradise. Therefore, and better by far than further exhortations, I will describe the place. It will conclude everything I have tried to say.

The spot was in the Kivu province lying to the east of the country now known as Zaire. I had never before been to what was then the Congo and at that time, freshly independent, the place was in a turmoil. The various game reserves, established by the Belgians, were in disarray. Poaching was rife. Money was not coming from the capital. Wardens were being shot, cars confiscated. I and some friends, notably the man already mentioned for his scarred and much-bitten body, wished to visit the Virunga volcanoes that lie in Kivu. It was an odd time to go—our passports vanished at the frontier—but there was, as we quickly realised, much recompense. On reflection there could scarcely have been a better time for visiting *Gorilla gorilla* upon a mountainside.

Once we had left the complexities, and were walking up the slopes leading away from them, we were in a wilderness. There is no other word. The former rules had vanished and the paths were overgrown. They were only wide where elephants and buffaloes had made recent use of them. I remember skidding magnificently, first on the mud and then on the bamboo when we reached its zone. Finally, soapy with sweat and panting in the thinner air of 10,000 feet, we came across a hut that the Belgians once had made. Someone had burned down half of it but in its other half, charred and open, we made a temporary home. From there we set forth to find our quarry.

It was exhausting work. Volcanoes have steep sides and up them we floundered in that hot thin air. At times, gasping with disbelief at my lack of energy, I would meet a handy tree, slump over a bough like a towel put out to dry, and hang there until I found some strength to move ahead once more. The trees were small, and mainly *Hagenia*. The rest of the vegetation was tall, with wild celery growing splendidly. Through this, and round the trees, we tracked the gorillas up and down that incredible countryside.

190

Gorillas live in family groups. Throughout each day they wander, pulling at the food, and leaving behind narrow swathes of paths. Around midday they each construct a nest. This can be on the ground or in the branches of a tree. In the afternoon the animals wander on once more, feeding, playing games if they are young, and filling in the time until evening comes. Then a more substantial nest is made by each of them, and in these comfortable beds they spend the night. For any tracker there is, in consequence, a sufficiency of clues. It is not easy at first deciding whether one pathway was made before another, or whether its trampled undergrowth was damaged earlier, but the nests were always a help. On waking in the morning each gorilla defecates into its bed, and these remains were often easier to age than the nests themselves. At all events we improved our tracking skills with time through all that celery, eventually knowing we must be very near.

The shriek was quite the loudest thing that I have ever heard. I was stunned. Every corpuscle in my blood seemed to halt at once. I felt a pain inside my chest. Gone was the heavy breathing of before. Gone, in fact, was breathing of any kind at all. I stayed where I was, turned abruptly into stone, and did not, could not, move an inch. The noise came again. This time, although no quieter than before, I was slightly more prepared. Instead of stiffening into immobility I began to think it might be wise, and even possible, to retreat a step or two. My friends were doing so and I crawled back with them. There were more noises, a crashing, a thrashing and soon a rapid smacking of fists beating upon a chest. Then came silence and the noise we made was all we heard as we softly crawled away. A *Hagenia* tree stood conveniently near and, with infinite care, we levered ourselves on to its easy limbs. We found further handholds and slowly climbed the tree. Until now we had seen no sign of our neighbours in all that undergrowth, the mountain gorilla, a creature not even recorded until this century.

Then, as we put up our arms to take another grip, we saw black arms doing the same some thirty yards away. Another *Hagenia*, just like our own, was suddenly full of them. There they were, and there we were, with both groups staring hard. 'Do nothing abrupt,' the books had said, and so we stayed, looking, wondering and considerably content. In time they relaxed their vigilance, pulled at plants and started eating again. In time we too could shift our stance, discover more comfortable spots and settle down to watch those splendid animals. What joy it was! What perfect happiness! We were in wilderness.